IDOLATRY MADE ME DO IT

IDOLATRY MADE ME DO IT

Kayla Fointno Richardson

Idolatry Made Me Do It

Copyright © 2026 by Kayla Fointno Richardson

All rights reserved.

Published By: Books By KJF Self-Publishing, LLC

www.booksbykjf.com

ISBN: 979-8-9897684-2-4 (Hardback)

ISBN: 979-8-9897684-3-1 (Paperback)

Library of Congress Control Number: 2026901726

Editor: Darian Nealy

Dedication

To the God that loved my idolatrous heart.

Thank you for dusting me off and making me new every time I crawled back to you in repentance. I could never repay you, so I vow to show you my gratitude with the way I live my life. I will choose you every day, forsaking all others.

To the people that will read this book.

I was crushed for this oil. This book came at a price. Jesus paid it first and I pay it every day—with my flesh.

To the children I have yet to bear and to the one that I have been blessed to inherit.

This is my legacy and this is your inheritance. I will slay Goliath, so you won't have to.

May this book transcend time and reach generations I will never see...

"Therefore, my beloved, flee from idolatry."
I Corinthians 10:14 (NKJV)

TABLE OF CONTENTS

What Exactly Did Idolatry Make You Do?

I'm glad you asked.

Let me start by saying: I, Kayla Fointno Richardson, am a born sinner. With God and you as my witness, I would like to ask God to forgive me for my idolatrous proclivities. Join me in repentance if you feel led...

In addition to my public repentance, I'd also like to highlight that while idolatry made me do it, I take full responsibility. I have been a rebellious, idolatrous whore according to Ezekiel 16:28 and Revelation 19:2 and in full transparency and in the spirit of honesty, I did not want to write this book. Like it says in Romans 2, do you tell people not to be an adulterer, yet you're an adulterer? Do you tell people not to be a liar, yet you are a liar? Working my way through the rubble of idolatry, I did not want to be a hypocrite; even now, I felt/feel so unworthy to speak about something of this magnitude. This is what the Bible says about me in 1 Samuel 15:23 (NKJV), "For rebellion is as the sin of witchcraft, and stubbornness is as iniquity and idolatry. Because you have rejected the word of the Lord, He also has rejected you from being king." In and out of rebellion, not choosing the Lord's side. On the opposite end of the spectrum, I also know that I come to you all as the least of these, as a sinner that has been saved by grace through faith. I'm not perfect and I don't proclaim to be. In my studies, I've found that what set David apart was His heart and his humility to repent. Evident in my life and throughout this process, I've tried to keep my heart pure and pliable; so again, I remind you, I am truly the least of these. I have no *right* to *write* a book about idolatry; but alas, here I am–a recipient of the grace of God.

You'll soon read about all the heinous things idolatry made me do to my God, my first love. But possibly the worst of all, idolatry made me almost forfeit my inheritance and my children's inheritance. Minding my business as I always do, randomly, someone addressed me with a word of the Lord. Exclaiming that I was sitting on my children's inheritance by not completing *this* book. Ironically, immediate conviction forced me into a chair, and as I sat and pondered on the words spoken, it didn't take long to realize the truth God had spoken through that person. My worship to pride coerced this manuscript writing process from a few months to one year to two years. In my pride, laced with stubbornness, I couldn't fathom that someone like *me* could write a book this powerful. I didn't know pride often masquerades as insecurity; thus, I didn't conceptualize that in my refusal to believe what God said about me, I was being prideful. It was disguised as humility, so I naturally fell for the deception. To God, the aroma that sailed past His nostrils was pride. Leviathan, the king of all pride (Job 41:34) was the god I bowed down to every time I didn't *feel* worthy enough to write this book. I idolized my feelings of unworthiness not realizing it was a cover for pride. But thank God for Jesus; because of Jesus, not only did I finish this book, but it's now in your hands, making your life better. With the blood of Jesus Christ, idolatry had to lose its hold on me. Yes, insecurity concerning my abilities as God's author will try to make a return, but now that I've overcome, the same authority that raised Jesus from the dead is on the inside of me to silence that prideful insecurity as I go forth and write. I'm free!

I will forever be sorrowful for the things idolatry made me do, but grateful for the experience–even more grateful for the testimony. Because of my testimony and the blood of the Lamb, I have overcome *him* (Satan). God has been gracious enough to deliver me–now I can help deliver you. As you near the end of this book, my hope is that you'll be clear on what exactly idolatry made *you* do.

As you read this book there are two prayers I'd like to be constantly on your lips:

"God, reveal to me all of my idols and idolatrous ways?"

"God, give me the strength to release them and choose you."

What Is Idolatry?

*"Now the works of the flesh are evident, which are: adultery, fornication, uncleanness, lewdness, **idolatry**, sorcery, hatred, contentions, jealousies, outbursts of wrath, selfish ambitions, dissensions, heresies, envy, murders, drunkenness, revelries, and the like; of which I tell you beforehand, just as I also told you in time past, that those who practice such things will not inherit the kingdom of God." Galatians 5:19-21 (NKJV)*

Idolatry is the worship of someone or something other than God– the father, son and the Holy Ghost. Idolatry can also be described as anything you love more than your obedience to God. God created us to worship Him, yet in our sinful nature, we are drawn to worship anything and everything. Idolatry gets in the way of God's natural order pertaining to the function in which He created us. As a God, jealous over His creation, idolatry presents a huge problem for Him. While the "Great Defender" never met a problem He couldn't solve, it nonetheless is the very thing that hinders the affection that is due Him from His creation. God is so passionate about having no other gods before Him that He put it on tablets and gave it to Moses to give to the Children of Israel. Making the theme of the first two commandments a warning about reverencing other gods.

Idolatry is a heart issue, more succinctly, an issue of what you love and worship. The thing or person you have made an idol is now the very thing you worship. Because idolatry is also a heart issue, oftentimes people try to remove the "things" or distance themselves from the person, when really it is the heart that needs healing. It is the heart that is wicked and lusting after a different god to serve. It's the heart that has grown black from a lack of asking God to search it for offensive ways (Psalms 139:23-24).

Indicators of Idolatry

As I journey to reveal to you what idolatry made *me* do, let me also paint a portrait that outlines the inner workings of idolatry. Idolatry is preceded by an anesthesia called deception. Deception is idolatry's secret service agent, turned friend because they lack ethical boundaries. Both live in the land of de-lulu (delusion), where deception constantly tells idolatry, "You're doing great sweetie, keep going. The people love you and everything is fine." Assuredly, they both work in tandem to tell us what our innately wicked hearts want to hear. Without deception, idolatry might have some boundaries; but, because deception is the hovering cloud, idolatry is free to roam. Deception also makes idolatry easier to digest. You ever wonder how people can actively live a homosexual lifestyle, yet preach, teach and/or proclaim the gospel, publicly? You ever wonder how someone can have multiple abortions and feel no remorse to God? Or how someone can curse at their husband or wife, even their children, yet use the same mouth to pray for the sick? How pastors can grace God's pulpit while sleeping with every member of their church, man or woman; never forgetting to mention their love for the first lady at the beginning of every sermon. How someone can declare they're a Christ-centered business yet lie on their taxes every year. All these examples are marked by idolatry with deception as the numbing agent. While I name these overt sins, I have no room to cast a stone as I was a prime candidate for idolatry, because I was born in a religious structure, adultery to another god was a part of the package. Most people I know with similar experiences to me usually never get their card pulled, doing just enough to "technically" make it into Heaven, but so displeasing to God.

Living ignorant of the destruction all around them, but not me; I was a called out one. God gave me up to a reprobate mind when I chose another god over Him. Thinking I was hearing His voice when really it was the voice of idolatry–sultrous and endearing. Asking God questions with corruption in my heart and receiving an answer my idolatry deserved (Ezekiel 14:4).

Indicator *You're* in Idolatry

Some indicators you're in idolatry is when *it* (only you can identify your "it") is all you can think about, when you wake up in the morning and before you go to bed at night. Another indicator you're in idolatry is if you would be devastated, almost inconsolable to lose it. Another indicator is if you have to sin to get it or keep it. A final indicator is if God is asking you for *it* and you cannot relinquish it. You make statements like, "I can surrender it, but..." or "I just don't see it as a problem..." If God asks you for it TODAY and there is a hesitation...that's an idol. You have placed another god before the Lord and His heart is grieved. I need you to know that even as I write this, it's nearly consuming me as well. I can't even imagine the countless things I do, even before noon on a normal day that grieve God's heart and show Him that I don't honor Him as my only God or His commandments. Nonetheless, sadness doesn't move the Father; action does–we need to repent and turn from our wicked ways. Before I get too ahead of myself, let's outline various things we can turn into idols or other gods in our lives:

Job, family, spouse, kids, money, grief, marriage, sexual immorality, bitterness/unforgiveness, pastors, leaders, social media, emotions, self, opinion, and so much more.

Why Idolatry Is (Inherently) Bad

At this point, I realize you still might not be convinced as to why idolatry is so unacceptable to God. Let's go back to the basics.

Idolatry is inherently bad because it worships another god and our God is jealous of his creation giving their worship to anything or anyone besides Him. Exodus 20:5 (NKJV) says "You shall not bow down to them nor serve them. For I, the Lord your God, am a jealous God, visiting the iniquity of the fathers upon the children to the third and fourth generations of those who hate Me." Understanding the character of the God that has given you your salvation might dispel a lot of disobedience we knowingly and unknowingly rehearse in our daily lives. It's also important to remember that idolatry is spiritual adultery. The same way your spouse would have a problem with you being unfaithful in your marriage is the same way God has a problem with you knowingly or unknowingly serving, loving, devoting time to another god. People who cheat on their spouse more than likely cheated on God well before their spouse. Adultery in the natural realm is an indication of adultery in the spiritual realm; if a person cannot be faithful to God, they could never be faithful to you.

Difference Between 1st and 2nd Commandments

1. You shall have no other gods before Me.

"You shall have no other gods before Me." Exodus 20:3 (NKJV)

2. You shall not make idols.

"You shall not make for yourself a carved image—any likeness of anything that is in heaven above, or that is in the earth beneath, or that is in the water under the earth; you shall not bow down to them nor serve them. For I, the Lord your God, am a jealous God, visiting the iniquity of the fathers upon the children to the third and fourth generations of those who hate Me, but showing mercy to thousands, to those who love Me and keep My commandments. Exodus 20:4-6 (NKJV)

These two commandments are often used interchangeably and may even feel redundant, so clarification of God's intent might be necessary. The first commandment explains the object of worship–only God. This commandment tells us *who* to worship. We are to only worship Yahweh. No other gods should compete for a place in our heart. The second commandment explains the practice of worship–forbidding carved images/ idols. This commandment tells us *how* to worship, not through man-made images or representations.

How do we idolize things, people, etc?

We make them bigger than God. We give these things attention or rank them in a place that should only be reserved for God. While we may not physically bow to most things, metaphorically, we bow every time we love *that thing* above God.

Biblical Evidence of Idolatry

If you've kept reading this far, maybe you're convinced, but like me, you thrive off Biblical evidence. Let's start with Leah. Idolizing a man, she named three of her babies out of the pain of being unloved by her husband. Reuben, "The LORD has seen my trouble, and now my husband will love me." Simeon, "The LORD has given me this son also, because he heard that I was not loved." Levi, "Now my husband will be bound more tightly to me, because I have borne him three sons" (See Genesis 29 & 30). It wasn't until the fourth one that she realized it was only the love of God she needed to survive. Judah, "Now I will praise the Lord." I won't delve too much into this topic, but the modern-day comparisons are uncanny. Women out of wedlock and within the confines of marriage are having children in hopes of winning the affection of a man. Holy Spirit speaking through Grandma always said, "A baby won't make that man love you or stay" and this reigns true whether you're helping to create the 12 tribes of Israel or having that man's 12th baby.

Another example of idolatry is David's idolatry of lust (see 2 Samuel 11). In His desire to obey the god of his flesh, it led to sexual immorality and murder to cover up the sexual immorality. This eventually not only cost him the kingdom, but he also passed this down to his son(s). David didn't kill the idol of lust, so it traveled on through his bloodline. Solomon was beloved but was more obedient to his lust than he was to God–he lost the kingdom. So many of us have compromised our future, our legacy to share our body with someone who was never meant to be or stay in our life. Like Solomon, you've fallen into sexual sin and now countless destiny destroying relationships have forced you so far out of the will of God you refuse to serve the Lord because *you* feel betrayed by love.

The last example I would like to use is Sarah and Abraham. They made their prophetic word an idol. God promised them an heir and when they didn't see the offspring that God promised them in Genesis 15, Sarai took Hagar, her slave, and made an illegitimate heir. Ishmael would prove to be a threat to the actual promise that would come years later. Many of us have prophetic words that we have contoured our lives just right so as to end up having the word "fall" into place. As if the Lord didn't tell us that He was watching *His* word to perform it (Jeremiah 1:12). Abraham and Sarah spent so much time making the prophetic word an idol that once they received it, naturally the prophetic word that manifested into a boy became their idol. So much so that God had to threaten to take it away so Abraham could decide in his heart who his god would be–his son or Yahweh.

This would be a good time to take an inventory on what's got a grip on you. What has your obedience instead of God?

Reward for Idolatry

"Therefore put to death your members which are on the earth: fornication, uncleanness, passion, evil desire, and covetousness, which is idolatry." Colossians 3:5 (NKJV)

Let's discuss the reward or the fruit for your idolatry. Don't be confused by the word, "reward." This is a reward that will make you wish you weren't an idolatrous whoremonger.

The first grand prize, a reprobate mind according to Romans 1:28 (KJV), "And even as they did not like to retain God in *their* knowledge, God gave them over to a reprobate mind, to do those things which are not convenient". I once heard someone say, a peace of mind *is* the grace of God. We don't know and possibly couldn't even imagine life if God were to take away His grace from us. His grace is like a coating of metal from the devourer. God taking His grace from us alone, would be enough to go insane. Ask King Saul. A reprobate or debased mind is nothing more than a mind free from the grace of God. An indicator is when convictions become less pressing. The Holy Spirit is quenched, our pulse for righteousness fades and we become numb to the sins that were once inconceivable.

The second grand prize, strong delusions according to 2 Thessalonians 2:11-12 (KJV)," And for this cause God shall send them strong delusion, that they should believe a lie: that they all might be damned who believed not the truth but had pleasure in unrighteousness". You ever wonder how someone can fully profess their unwavering love for God yet be so steeped in sin– a strong delusion and this is a person not worth arguing with. Only intercession and an act from a merciful God will overturn this level of delusion.

The final grand prize is similar to the second, but with a cherry on top. Isaiah 66:4 (NKJV), "So will I choose their delusions, And bring their fears on them; Because, when I called, no one answered,

When I spoke, they did not hear; But they did evil before My eyes, And chose that in which I do not delight". This reward is a combo: strong delusions and fears–being delusional and fearful is possibly the worst combination. The sad thing about this tag team is that pride probably has this person wrapped so tightly they don't even think to ask for mercy. They've forgotten that as a child of the most high, they can ask for forgiveness and their Father would be faithful to forgive; not to withhold their consequences, but to forgive. An Abrahamic plea for mercy from Genesis 18 is necessary here or even Daniel's prayer from Daniel 9 would help the chances of defeating this twin army.

*For a bonus prize read Ezekiel 14:3-5.

Hope for Turning from Idolatrous Ways

I alluded to it when I explained some indicators of idolatry and in the third grand prize, but there is hope. There is a way to turn from your idolatrous ways. Once repentance has been offered and cognizant changes have been made, what can't the God of the universe do for a repentant heart. This is what differentiated David from any other man, any other king. He knew how to fall on his face in repentance to God. He understood the importance of humility. All God is looking for is a humble and contrite heart (Psalms 51). This is the type of heart that even with spots of inequities, God would go on to birth our savior, Jesus Christ through this bloodline. This is the type of heart that God would covenant Himself to and promise to protect (2 Samuel 7). David turned from his idolatrous ways and while the consequences still met up to him, God spared *his* life and didn't allow the enemy to take all the tribes in the Kingdom of Israel. When Leah decided to focus on God and not the idol of her husband, she was able to name a baby out of her worship to God instead of her pain. Leah and David are proof that we can never out give God. Once we give Him our whole hearts and turn from the thing we chose to worship in His place, He restores, he makes it as if it never happened. He remembers it no more and requests that we only remember when it's time to share our testimony.

This is another great time to take inventory of your life. Ask God to search your heart for any idols you have set up in your heart before Him. Maybe you don't have a golden calf made from jewelry like the children of Israel, but what is your modern-day equivalent? You don't have to stay bound, but you *do* have a choice to make.

Altar vs. Altar

If you decide to move forward and rid yourself of idolatry, after your initial repentance, maintenance from idolatry will be vital for your deliverance. It's necessary to ask God daily to search your heart (Psalms 139:23-24). "God, are there any idolatrous ways in me?" It is constant work to keep your heart pure from worshiping someone or something other than God. It's also important to ask God to destroy any altars spiritually or naturally you might have built to any idols in your life. Example: Have you ever been to a store, restaurant or nail shop and you see candles, pictures, statues and more on a table—that's a physical altar, a place of worship to a god (It's also important to note that all your money is going to that altar. It's almost like every time you eat at that place or get your nails done at that place, you are paying your tithes to that god). In some cultural contexts this could be considered a shrine. Altars and shrines have slight differences, nonetheless, both condemned by God. Even more practical: a room or space dedicated to sports apparel, a room or space dedicated to sorority or fraternity paraphernalia, the list goes on. These things, whether a literal altar or spiritual altar, need to be taken down and an altar to the Lord needs to be rebuilt in its place. Once they are taken down you will need to ask God for His forgiveness for building this altar and for making sacrifices at that altar. A new altar to the Lord might look like an invisible altar of thanksgiving (using all of God's name, e.g. "Thank you Jehovah Jireh. Thank you for being my Jehovah Shalom, etc.") or an altar of praise in your home that goes before the Lord every day. This new altar you build will be where you symbolically lay idols, Ungodly ambitions, unforgiveness and so much more as you consecrate yourself to God. As you read this book, I will go in depth about a few things idolatry made me do and about the altars I built to feed my idols. While my natural sin nature aided in these idolatrous dealings, I take full responsibility in my corporation to live boldly in my sins. My hope is that you will see yourself in some of these idolatrous mirrors and that you too will surrender the idols on God's altar to be burned, clearing up the space in your heart for its rightful owner, El Elyon, the most high God. Either God's altar will stand tall or the altar of idols will be destroyed–as Elijah.

Idolatry of Self

"Satanists don't believe in worshiping the devil, they simply just believe in putting themselves above everyone else." -Alyssa Nwanne

"But know this, that in the last days perilous times will come: For men will be <u>lovers of themselves</u>, lovers of money, boasters, proud, blasphemers, disobedient to parents, unthankful, unholy, unloving, unforgiving, slanderers, without self-control, brutal, despisers of good, traitors, headstrong, haughty, lovers of pleasure rather than lovers of God, having a form of godliness but denying its power. And from such people turn away!" 2 Timothy 3:1-5 (NKJV)

How many people do you know that have at least one of the traits? Now, how many of these traits do *you* possess?

The first word that comes to my spirit when I think of lovers of self is the term, "Selfie." While this term or action of taking a selfie is not inherently negative, it comes with a derogatory last-minute thought that identifies *oneself*. Disclaimer, I am not saying all who take selfies are lovers of themselves–I love a good selfie. I especially love a good selfie if the world has tried to tear down your confidence since childhood. With each picture snapped, finally you're taking some of that power back–good for you! What I am saying is, at times what selfies represent can be indicative of the last days. On the other hand, maybe you're like me and you don't over-indulge in selfies or struggle with being a lover of self. Here's a revelation that the Holy Spirit showed me. Being a lover of self is also lying to protect your image. E.g. telling everyone you were stuck in traffic to avoid being judged or persecuted when really you have poor time management skills and you were just running late. This is a form of toxic self-preservation; you made an error and now it is being covered up to "save face." This is not to be confused with preservation of self in an unsafe relationship, whether parental, platonic or significant other, etc.

Before we move on, I want to home in on a couple examples from the Bible of how toxic self-preservation became idolatry of self, focusing in on Abraham and Issac. Two men–father and son, at two different points in history, traveling to places *God* sent them, with no reason to fear or lie, chose to be dishonest. Ironically, lying to the same ruler, Abimelech, king of Gerar and potentially sacrificing their wife's honor to protect and elevate themselves. This dishonesty not only traveled through their lineage but showed its ugly head in their marriages as well. First Abraham lied in Genesis 12 and in Genesis 20; both times endangering his wife, Sara(i)h. It's important to note, this idolatry of self comes with lying, manipulation, coercion, sickness and disease.

"And it came to pass, when he was close to entering Egypt, that he said to Sarai his wife, "Indeed I know that you are a woman of beautiful countenance. Therefore it will happen, when the Egyptians see you, that they will say, 'This is his wife'; and they will kill me, but they will let you live. Please say you are my sister, that it may be well with me for your sake, and that I may live because of you." But the Lord plagued Pharaoh and his house with great plagues because of Sarai, Abram's wife. And Pharaoh called Abram and said, "What is this you have done to me? Why did you not tell me that she was your wife? Why did you say, 'She is my sister'? I might have taken her as my wife. Now therefore, here is your wife; take her and go your way."" Genesis 12:11-13, 17-19 (NKJV)

Unfortunately, Abraham hadn't dealt with his natural tendency to lie so this happens again in Genesis 20.

Reflection: If the father of our faith (Abraham) struggled with the truth, how much more do we need the Holy Spirit to walk in integrity?

"Now Abraham said of Sarah his wife, "She is my sister." And Abimelech king of Gerar sent and took Sarah. But God came to Abimelech in a dream by night, and said to him, "Indeed you are a dead man because of the woman whom you have taken, for she is a man's wife." But Abimelech had not come near her; and he said, "Lord, will You slay a righteous nation also? Did he not say to me, 'She is my sister'? And she, even she herself said, 'He is my brother.' In the integrity of my heart and innocence of my hands I have done this."" *Genesis 20:2-5 (NKJV)*

"And Abimelech called Abraham and said to him, "What have you done to us? How have I offended you, that you have brought on me and on my kingdom a great sin? You have done deeds to me that ought not to be done." Then Abimelech said to Abraham, "What did you have in view, that you have done this thing?" And Abraham said, "Because I thought, surely the fear of God is not in this place; and they will kill me on account of my wife." *Genesis 20:9-11 (NKJV)*

Could Abraham's second time lying to preserve himself be the continuance of a generational pattern as years later Issac does the same thing his father did?

"And the men of the place asked about his wife. And he said, "She is my sister"; for he was afraid to say, "She is my wife," because he thought, "lest the men of the place kill me for Rebekah, because she is beautiful to behold." Then Abimelech called Isaac and said, "Quite obviously she is your wife; so how could you say, 'She is my sister'?" Isaac said to him, "Because I said, 'Lest I die

on account of her.'" And Abimelech said, "What is this you have done to us? One of the people might soon have lain with your wife, and you would have brought guilt on us."" Genesis 26:7, 9-10 (NKJV)

In Genesis 27, Rebekah and Jacob lie to get the blessing from Issac before he could bestow it upon Esau. In Genesis 29 we even see that Rebecca's brother Laban chose dishonesty when he gave Leah to Jacob in marriage, first, instead of Rachel. Despite Laban and Jacob having a verbal agreement that Jacob would work seven years for Rachel.

Collective sigh

Take a moment to breathe and assess life. If lying to preserve your name's sake and to maintain the public's perception of you is landing too close to home, I want you to know it's okay–I've been there. Repent for loving yourself more than your obedience to God's commandments and turn from those wicked ways. Warning: this takes a lot of humility. I'm praying God will give you grace to begin to live without the idol of self, especially in a world that tells you a life with idols is normal. Remember, just because it's normal doesn't mean it's healthy.

A Heart Only a Father Could Love (Inadequacy)

Something that also causes an idol of self is inadequacy. In general, inadequacy originates from several places, but my first-hand experience of inadequacy came in through rejection, via a breakup. This inadequacy tore through the soft tissue of my heart, eventually turning it to stone. That stone brought a Lucifer fall type of jealousy that tormented me with every thought. I began to care about how I was being perceived, how I dressed, the life I could portray, I was growing superficial as the days carried on. I couldn't compliment people or congratulate them. Comparison became my oxygen tank, and jealousy became my nasal cannula. Only God could still love a heart like that. That's when He wrote me this letter and the heart surgery began:

Your healing is important to me, Kayla. That man hurt you and he took a piece of you. It was undetectable, but I know. I know all your inner workings. A small light that no one would recognize, but I do. I know. I feel it because you're made in my image and now because that piece was taken, we don't match. I want you to have that piece back. I'm reclaiming it for you. You are worthy. You could go on to this next relationship and eventually get married with this piece missing–no one would know the difference. But like the story of the ten lepers in Luke 17, your gratitude has made you whole while others are satisfied with just being cleansed. As your Heavenly bridegroom, I want you to have your complete healing. There is more where that came from. I WILL BLESS YOU IN FRONT OF HIM with a man that won't need options–it'll be only you! Stay encouraged and don't let yourself get lonely. Trust me that BEFORE THE YEAR IS OUT, I will do this for you! Wait on me, I say! And be of good courage. I've started this desire–I will fulfill it. Don't focus on the when. Take these next seven days to pray and fast. Seek me with everything you have.

Before you begin, I want to tell you what you're up against. Because of what happened, rejection has brought on a spirit of inadequacy. That's why when someone else is spotlighted, jealousy shows up. You feel inadequate. Surrender that to me.

God wrote me this letter in January of 2024, and it wouldn't be until July of 2024 that I would have the courage to fast in order to get to the root of where this jealousy initiated. I did the fast and it felt like nothing changed. In fact, I had awakened jealousy in my heart like never before and I didn't know how to get rid of it. I prayed the jealousy away and it didn't go. I rebuked the jealousy and it mocked me, only to get even more aggressive. Just as I was giving up, I stumbled upon this letter, and it clicked. Finally, I saw the root of jealousy—inadequacy. As I began to take an ax to the root of jealousy (inadequacy) in prayer, I declared in faith that jealousy was gone. I got on social media to test the theory and finally, I was able to rejoice with those who rejoiced (Romans 12:15).

A couple things I want to unpack here: Whenever you're fasting. A true biblical definition of fasting means to abstain from all foods and sometimes water for a period of time. Not what the world tells you to do, appeasing your flesh like fasting from tv, social media, your phone, people, "your kids/spouse", premarital sex, etc. There is a difference between consecration and fasting. Some stubborn strongholds *only* respond to *fasting* and killing of the flesh. Sometimes spirits lay dormant, waiting for the right time to show themselves and ruin your life. When you fast, in God's mercy, He shines a light, (Isaiah 58:8. *Light;* meaning knowledge) bringing to surface whatever certificate of death had your name on it so you can use the power God gave you to decree a thing so it can be established (See Isaiah 58 on how to Biblically fast).

Jealousy came out with guns blazing because I was bringing it to the surface by fasting. Jealousy had a plan to ruin my marriage at its inception and possibly even a few friendships–of course it was upset that I was uncovering its hiding spot. While I had the right passion, unfortunately, throughout my whole fast I had no spiritual tools to take its neck off until God, in His mercy, led me to knowledge. When what's lying dormant begins to surface, it makes one feel defeated. This is when most stop fasting before it's time or speak death against a fast, they just completed by saying, "The fast didn't work." This is the worst time to stop fasting. This is good news–you have lured the fish in, now you just need the right hook to catch it for good. Additionally, I knew not to stop fasting, or to speak against my time fasting, but I didn't know why jealousy wasn't leaving. I searched for legal rights and all points of entry. I didn't realize I was casting out the wrong thing. It was like cutting off a flower and expecting it not to grow back. As long as the root was still active, that flower was coming back in another season. The spirit of jealousy was just the fruit of a bigger covert root. It wasn't until I cast out the source or control center of jealousy that I was able to destroy it. Same with a strongman. Killing the strongholds will exhaust you because they keep coming back, but killing the strongman, there is your victory. I talk about this in another chapter, but I'll reference it here: every strongman is like an octopus. One tentacle might be pride, one might be lust, one might be jealousy, one might be bitterness. Cutting off one or multiple tentacles won't kill the octopus. Only until I reach the heart of that octopus will it be dead. That's essentially what I was doing, praying and rebuking a tentacle–jealousy. Not knowing I was only praying against the tip of the iceberg, ignorant of the fact that there was a deeper root of inadequacy that was attached to the mother of all roots: rejection. Confused with God because fasting and praying "didn't work", when really, I didn't use, nor have the biblical tools and principles given in His word to see a victory.

Self-Sabotaging

Another form of idolatry of self is self-sabotage; personally, placing obstacles in your own walkway. Creating problems out of nothing or as the old folks would say, "Making mountains out of molehills." Committing to *this* kind of idolatry results in your allegiance to standing in your own way over what God has said about you, and it is now separating you from your promise. You are more obedient to the infirmity of self than to the spirit that raised Jesus from the dead on the inside of you (Romans 8:11). The carnality of your mind is enmity against God (Roman 8:7). *You* are the very enemy of your soul. You are the very thing you ask God to defeat, but because of free will and dominion, God won't interfere with what He gave *you* the power to dominate and overcome. He is a *just* God, whether His *justice* benefits you or not. A great example of self-sabotage is the children of Israel. Before you aggressively shake your head in agreement, if you were in that number back in that Bible Day, you would be right along with the children of Israel. Giving your gold chains and wedding rings to Aaron just like everyone else–don't lie to me, lie to ya mama, but I've digressed. These people constantly sabotaged what God wanted to do for and through them. They complained and when they weren't complaining, they were worshiping *everything* other than God. The mark of a person that self-sabotages is the oblivion to their own self-sabotage. When they are finally made aware, the rumination of their self-sabotaging makes them do it even more. This is followed by an activation of victim mode, in which they lean into their crutches even harder. Often sticking out a crutch to capture others to join their army of sabotage. Chances are they're of a lineage that has an iniquity of self-sabotaging. If not, they're the first, but unfortunately, they won't be the last.

On the other hand, you have a remnant of people that ask God to help them learn how to *not* ruin every good thing that happens in their life. You have the people that ask God to reveal to them the root of why they self-sabotage and when it started. This is the remnant that is called to take an ax to the tree of self-sabotage in valiant efforts to tear down and root up. Casting down imaginations, and every high thing that exalteth itself against the knowledge of God and bringing into captivity every thought to the obedience of Christ (2 Corinthians 10:5 KJV). This remnant sees the move of God in their life and begins to thrive in areas they used to barely survive in. This remnant gets this revelation and at the very smell of self-sabotage in another person they are grieved. Knowing the dark path their fellow brother or sister is on and praying the same grace of light God exposed on their infirmity to their neighbor. At first glance, we might think self-sabotaging isn't harmful, but it was so dangerous that God wouldn't let a generation of the Israelites into the promised land because of it. What promised land will you not be able to see because of self-sabotage? As a mental health therapist, I'm grateful for the theories that teach us how to reframe our thinking and that aid in the diminishing of self-sabotaging, but as a believer *and* a therapist, I advocate a little harder for us to look to the rule book of real "how to" examples that God gave us.

<u>Let's look at Job:</u>

The enemy's first trick is always to inspire us into self-sabotage. In scripture, we see where he encouraged Job to self-sabotage. He planned for Job to "curse God and die" (Job 2:9), but God had an expected end for Job (Psalms 62:5-6). God had a wager set on Job's faith. He made an investment in Job's faithfulness and obedience even unto a near death experience. The enemy's plan was for Job to come out of agreement with God's investment. Either we believe God in James chapter one concerning various trials or we don't. In a time of demonic pressure, Job was about to curse his way out of a double blessing. That's why we must resist Satan and he *will* flee. You are probably in a similar boat as Job, but please don't sabotage your Job chapter 42 because of *planned* adversity from your Job chapter 1.

SN: In our lives we can also see a pattern here. Satan attacks us in every area his short little arms can reach. This is proof that when calamity hits all around us, Satan isn't after those things being attacked–he is after our faith.

I want to take a moment from my writing process and encourage the person who, like Job, is tempted with giving up. You've been influenced to, "curse God and die" several times by several different people, and you're probably wondering how many Job 2:10 (NKJV) responses you have left *"But he said to her, 'You speak as one of the foolish women speaks. Shall we indeed accept good from*

God, and shall we not accept adversity?' In all this Job did not sin with his lips." Satan is pitching everything he can at you, but I need you to take heart because there has been a conversation that has taken place in the courtroom of Heaven concerning your destiny. God gambled your *inability* to never stop loving Him and He has bet on your faith to be immovable. The king of pride thinks your knees will buckle and you will faint. *I've come to declare over you that you will NOT faint, you will NOT grow weary, you will NOT lose heart. I speak supernatural strength to every part of your soul and body. I speak a fresh wind to carry you to the finish line. I call your warring angels to the scene, and I ask that Jehovah Gibbor, have His way, in Jesus' name, amen!* So, take heart because your lines have fallen in pleasant (Psalms 16:6). Spoiler alert, on the other end of self-sabotaging is full confidence in who God has created you to be. You come out on the other end better than you were before. Dare I say like the three Hebrew boys–without a trace of the fire you were living in. Keep going, don't look back, stop questioning "why you." You cannot stop here. You're too close to victory. Your faith has qualified you and your faith will carry you. *Selah.*

We can learn a lot of strategies from the book of Job:

1. The enemy is never after the things he attacks–he's after your faith. The enemy wanted Job's faithfulness and allegiance to God. Upon hopefully obtaining that, he went after his family, his health, his relationships. Does this sound familiar? Think back to when all hell is breaking loose. Think on past attacks (or current) to your relationships, to your health, experiencing death of those closest to you. Your faith in God is tested, with every blow; with every, "If it ain't one thing, it's another..." Your faith in God is diminishing. Knowing without faith it's impossible to please God (Hebrews 11:6), knowing that God asks us to do things in faith without doubting because a double-minded man will receive nothing from God (See James 1), and ultimately knowing that we are saved by grace,

through *faith* (Ephesians 2:8). Satan is very crafty about his ways, but we are not ignorant of his devices (2 Corinthians 2:11).

2. Satan will use the people in your life to enable you to self-sabotage. Job's wife was used by Satan to further his agenda. I do however feel like we often forget that she too lost all her children, property, servants, etc. She was grieving just as much as Job. While this was no excuse for her to encourage or influence her husband to, "curse God and die." This is good context when discussing Job and his wife as well as an example of what it looks like when the plans of Satan manifest and he is successful at snatching a person's faith.

<u>Next, let's look at Zacharias:</u>

The angel of the Lord completely shut this man's mouth. God knew he would speak against the promised heir, so the angel shut Zacharias' mouth (See Luke 1). I'll pause here for anyone that wants to ask God for that same anointing (my advice, rather than making you mute for a period of time like Zacharias, possibly ask Him for a remix. That "think before you speak" anointing). Imagine if God would have not used the angel Gabriel to shut Zacharias' mouth? Zacharias would have killed the seed or the faith of the very thing he and his wife fervently believed God for. In God's mercy, did He make Zacharias mute. There would have still been a John the Baptist because God is sovereign, but what would have happened if God had not intervened? More than likely, Zacharias would have self-sabotaged not only His promise, but his wife's promise as well. Who else is your self-sabotaging affecting?

With the fruit of our self-sabotage in our hand, we still decide to blame the devil for our woes. Giving him too much radio time, we go on about how incorrigible he is, blind to the fact that he's not omnipresent. He simply roams, planting seeds and watches us water them as he visits his next believer. With every seed, our unbelief in God flourishes. Not realizing this would all be null and void if idolatry was killed. If you made a conscious decision to believe what God said about you. More importantly, stand in who God says you are when the enemy comes with seeds of a false identity. If you allow Satan to identify you, in his perversion, he will. So, remember the identity *God* gave you. You're royalty, you are chosen (1 Peter 2:9), you are a new creation (2 Corinthians 5:17), you are Christ-filled (Galatians 2:20), you are His workmanship (Ephesians 2:10), you are a friend of God (John 15:15), you are created in the image of God (Genesis 1:27), and you are a child of God (John 1:12), God's beloved, a true King's kid! Never forget who you are. Let this identity respond when the double-mindedness of self-sabotage speaks.

What are some patterns of sabotage in your life?

____

____

____

____

____

____

____

Strategy to stop self-sabotaging:

- Identifying the root cause and patterns

- Challenging negative self-talk

- Celebrate the small wins

- Practice compassion

- Set realistic goals

- Accountability

Choose a few strategies or create your own. Whatever you decide, self-sabotaging must end:

____

____

____

____

____

____

____

____

If You Love Me, Keep My Commandments

'"If you love Me, keep My commandments."' John 14:15 (NKJV)

"If you love me, keep my commandments." Such a simple statement yet loaded with complexities. Not because of the one who wrote it, but because of the ones who He wrote it for. Is it just me or does this "if" that rolls off Jesus' tongue kind of sting. It's almost provocative in the shocking sense that we have options. He didn't say, "because you love me..." or "since you love me...". The "if" speaks to the very nature of love, the nature of God, because God is love. While I'm grateful for a sovereign God that gave us options, I'm concerned because what exactly was Jesus implying in this "if." What other options are people choosing? This reiterates the statement and question combo that Mary, Mary stated so eloquently, yet gangsta, gangsta in one of their songs, "I love God, you don't love God? What's wrong with you?"

My next thought is more rudimentary in simply finding the antonym of love, hate. Because hate is the opposite of love, Jesus essentially said, if you don't keep my commandments, you hate me. Jesus immediately translates the lack of love to hate, what an even greater devastating blow because, "Of course I love you, Jesus". It's interesting how love is mentioned approx. 300+ times in the Bible, yet we just can't seem to get it right. As this verse permeated every corner of my mind, the Lord began to give me revelation.

First, Let's Define What Is Love:

God is Love

"He who does not love does not know God, for God is love." 1 John 4:8 (NKJV)

Love is Obedient

"If you love Me, keep My commandments." John 14:15 (NKJV)

"For this is the love of God, that we keep His commandments. And His commandments are not burdensome." 1 John 5:3 (NKJV)

Love is Sacrificial

"For God so loved the world, that he gave his only begotten Son, that whosoever believeth in him should not perish, but have everlasting life." John 3:16 (KJV)

"This is how we know what love is: Jesus Christ laid down his life for us. And we ought to lay down our lives for our brothers and sisters." 1 John 3:16 (NIV)

"Greater love has no one than this, than to lay down one's life for his friends." John 15:13 (NKJV)

Love is Superior

"And above all these put on love, which binds everything together in perfect harmony." Colossians 3:14 (ESV)

"So now faith, hope, and love abide, these three; but the greatest of these is love." 1 Corinthians 13:13 (ESV)

Love is a Verb

"Dear children, let's not merely say that we love each other; let us show the truth by our actions." 1 John 3:18 (NLT)

Love is a Way of Being

"And walk in love, as Christ also has loved us and given Himself for us, an offering and a sacrifice to God for a sweet-smelling aroma." Ephesians 5:2 (NKJV)

Love Has No Fear

"There is no fear in love; but perfect love casts out fear, because fear involves torment. But he who fears has not been made perfect in love." 1 John 4:18 (NKJV)

Love Prays for Enemies

"But I tell you, love your enemies and pray for those who persecute you." Matthew 5:44 (NIV)

Love Covers

"And above all things have fervent love for one another, for "love will cover a multitude of sins." 1 Peter 4:8 (NKJV)

"Hatred stirs up strife, but love covers all offenses." Proverbs 10:12 (ESV)

Love Is:

"Love is patient, love is kind. It does not envy, it does not boast, it is not proud. It does not dishonor others, it is not self-seeking, it is not easily angered, it keeps no record of wrongs. Love does not delight in evil but rejoices with the truth. It always protects, always trusts, always hopes, always perseveres. Love never fails. But where there are prophecies, they will cease; where there are tongues, they will be stilled; where there is knowledge, it will pass away." 1 Corinthians 13:4-8 (NIV)

Next, Let's Outline What His Commandments Are:

1. You Shall Have No Other Gods Before Me.

"You shall have no other gods before Me." Exodus 20:3 (NKJV)

2. You Shall Not Make Idols.

"You shall not make for yourself a carved image—any likeness of anything that is in heaven above, or that is in the earth beneath, or that is in the water under the earth; you shall not bow down to them nor serve them. For I, the Lord your God, am a jealous God, visiting the iniquity of the fathers upon the children to the third and fourth generations of those who hate Me, but showing mercy to thousands, to those who love Me and keep My commandments. Exodus 20:4-6 (NKJV)

3. You Shall Not Take the Name of the LORD Your God in Vain.

"You shall not take the name of the Lord your God in vain, for the Lord will not hold him guiltless who takes His name in vain." Exodus 20:7 (NKJV)

4. Remember the Sabbath Day, to Keep it Holy.

"Remember the Sabbath day, to keep it holy. Six days you shall labor and do all your work, but the seventh day is the Sabbath of the Lord your God. In it you shall do no work: you, nor your son, nor your daughter, nor your male servant, nor your female servant, nor your cattle, nor your stranger who is within your gates. For in six days the Lord made the heavens and the earth, the sea, and all that is in them, and rested the seventh day. Therefore, the Lord blessed the Sabbath day and hallowed it." Exodus 20:8-11 (NKJV)

5. Honor Your Father and Your Mother.

"Honor your father and your mother, that your days may be long upon the land which the Lord your God is giving you." Exodus 20:12 (NKJV)

6. You Shall Not Murder.

"You shall not murder." Exodus 20:13 (NKJV)

7. You Shall Not Commit Adultery.

"You shall not commit adultery." Exodus 20:14 (NKJV)

8. You Shall Not Steal.

"You shall not steal." Exodus 20:15 (NKJV)

9. You Shall Not Bear False Witness Against Your Neighbor.

"You shall not bear false witness against your neighbor." Exodus 20:16 (NKJV)

10. You Shall Not Covet.

"You shall not covet your neighbor's house; you shall not covet your neighbor's wife, nor his male servant, nor his female servant, nor his ox, nor his donkey, nor anything that is your neighbor's." Exodus 20:3-17 (NKJV)

<u>Here are these same commandments outlined in the new testament:</u>

1. You Shall Have No Other Gods Before Me.

"'And you shall love the Lord your God with all your heart, with all your soul, with all your mind, and with all your strength.' This is the first commandment. And the second, like it, is this: 'You shall love your neighbor as yourself.' There is no other commandment greater than these." Mark 12:30-31 (NKJV)

2. You Shall Not Make Idols.

"And do not become idolaters as were some of them. As it is written, 'The people sat down to eat and drink, and rose up to play.' Nor let us commit sexual immorality, as some of them did, and in one day twenty-three thousand fell; nor let us tempt Christ, as some of them also tempted, and were destroyed by serpents; nor complain, as some of them also complained, and were destroyed by the destroyer." 1 Corinthians 10:7-10 (NKJV)

3. You Shall Not Take the Name of the LORD Your God in Vain.

"But I say to you, do not swear at all: neither by heaven, for it is God's throne; nor by the earth, for it is His footstool; nor by Jerusalem, for it is the city of the great King. Nor shall you swear by your head, because you cannot make one hair white or black. But let your 'Yes' be 'Yes,' and your 'No,' 'No.' For whatever is more than these is from the evil one." Matthew 5:34-37 (NKJV)

4. Remember the Sabbath Day, to Keep it Holy.

"And He said to them, 'The Sabbath was made for man, and not man for the Sabbath. Therefore the Son of Man is also Lord of the Sabbath.'" Mark 2:27-28 (NKJV)

5. Honor Your Father and Your Mother.

"Children, obey your parents in the Lord, for this is right. 'Honor your father and mother,' which is the first commandment with promise: 'that it may be well with you and you may live long on the earth.'" Ephesians 6:1-3 (NKJV)

6. You Shall Not Murder.

"But let none of you suffer as a murderer, a thief, an evildoer, or as a busybody in other people's matters." 1 Peter 4:15 (NKJV)

7. You Shall Not Commit Adultery.

"Marriage is honorable among all, and the bed undefiled; but fornicators and adulterers God will judge." Hebrews 13:4 (NKJV)

8. You Shall Not Steal.

"Let him who stole steal no longer, but rather let him labor, working with his hands, what is good, that he may have something to give him who has need." Ephesians 4:28 (NKJV)

9. You Shall Not Bear False Witness Against Your Neighbor.

"Do not lie to one another, since you have put off the old man with his deeds, and have put on the new man who is renewed in knowledge according to the image of Him who created him." Colossians 3:9-10 (NKJV)

10. You Shall Not Covet.

"Let your conduct be without covetousness; be content with such things as you have. For He Himself has said, 'I will never leave you nor forsake you.'" Hebrews 13:5 (NKJV)

"For this you know, that no fornicator, unclean person, nor covetous man, who is an idolater, has any inheritance in the kingdom of Christ and God." Ephesians 5:5 (NKJV)

If We Say We Love God, Why Can't We Keep His Commandments?

From sexual self-pleasure, to his and her sinks, we have created accommodations around our selfishness. Because sin entered the world, our innate fleshly desire is to be selfish. The number one place we see selfishness is in relationships: platonic, family, and romantic alike. Romantically speaking, people often base the success of relationships on what one person can do for the other. Using relationships to fill voids that were not met well before the relationship began. Thinking, the other person is going to be their superhero and lover wrapped up into one. Placing unrealistic and unspoken expectations on *one* person. Fleeing at the first sight of their humanity. Forgetting that by nature of entering into a relationship, we are essentially saying, "I'm ready to serve this person," especially if it's to be a Godly relationship possibly on the road to covenant one day. Godly relationships are beginning to look like the world's relationships: "Me, me, me" and "I, I, I." When in reality, God set up relationships around the structural frame of, "We, we, we" and "Us, us, us." 1 Corinthians 7:3-4 is very clear about the selfless way relationships should be structured. If the man is serving the woman and the woman is serving the man, everyone is taken care of. This type of effort hosts an imaginary contract that promotes you to another level of servanthood. When these relationships don't work out, it's sometimes because one or both parties underestimated the amount of service it took to love and commit to someone.

In addition to the underestimated amount of service, one or both parties also might have failed to show love in their partner's language, rather in their own. While this world has now become hyper aware of *love languages*, we have yet to fully grasp how to take that awareness into action. What often happens is we love people in the love language *we* desire to be loved in, rather than the language our partner *needs* or has requested love in.

<u>Let's take Trey, for example:</u>

Trey's love language is physical touch, but his wife, True, would rather give him words of affirmation because that's what she's comfortable with. While Trey appreciates his wife's encouragement, he is often left feeling neglected because *his* love tank is not being filled up. One day they might get into an argument. Trey might say, "I'm not feeling very loved by you." To which his wife True might respond by saying, "What do you mean? I'm always complimenting you. I constantly love on you." True might even add, "Well, I don't really feel loved by you either." Trey might respond, "What do you mean, I'm always giving you hugs and kisses." Here we have a couple that are victims of a love deficit, whilst also the culprits of a selfish love. Trey wants to be hugged and kissed so he gives this to his wife, in turn making her feel unloved. True wants to be encouraged, she wants Trey to tell her how beautiful she is and what a great job as a wife she's doing, so she gives this to her husband, in turn making him feel unloved. Like two ships passing through the night.

All hope is not lost: If Trey and True are serious about keeping their covenant intact, they can make the necessary changes. It will require them to step out of themselves and out of their comfort zones. It might make Trey uncomfortable to exhort True with words and it might make True uncomfortable to give her husband at least 12 hugs a day, but this will take their love from a selfish love to a selfless love.

This is often how we are with God. We swear up and down we *love* God, but like Trey and True, God doesn't feel the love. We tend to love God in a way that suits us best, in a way that is most comfortable for us, and in the way *we* desire love. We have yet to keep one of God's commandments, so naturally, He has equated that to us not loving Him. Maybe you have murdered someone physically, but you kill your child's spirit everyday with harsh language. Maybe you haven't committed adultery, but you lust after those that you are not in covenant with. We have yet to cover, to be sacrificial, or be obedient. We're stuck in fear, being sedentary, and hating our enemies. God translates this failure to meet His expectation of love as hate. Declaring our love for God comes with contingencies; the declaration of our love is null and void until we keep and obey *His* commandments. Clanging symbols (1 Corinthians 13:1) is how I would venture to describe our frivolous declarations of love found on apparel, bumper stickers, written in and on notebooks, opening lines to every award acceptance speech, etc. It's sad really, a world full of His own creation and we have yet to master how to best *love* our creator. I believe God is ready to show us how to *love Him* properly–we just have to be willing. We must step outside of our self-centered society. While this is indicative of the times (2 Timothy 3:2), we must strive to choose a love that puts God or our neighbors above ourselves. The best way to learn this is through God's example. He teaches us how to love Him and those around us. Perfect in all His ways, giving His only son on a *"maybe,"* we would give our lives to Him for salvation. He loved us on a *"maybe."* Maybe we turn from our wicked ways and confess that Jesus is Lord. Maybe even after we were saved by faith, through grace we would choose to only serve Him and forsake all the idols of this world. Just maybe... Oh what love!

How Do You Keep His Commandments

"And I will pray the Father, and he shall give you another Comforter, that he may abide with you forever." John 14:16 (KJV)

Obedience is the love language of God. As I learn more about the trinity and the significance of the Holy Spirit's role in our lives. At times I feel like we treat the Holy Spirit like Cinderella. Calling on Him when I need something but putting Him back on the shelf when He's not relevant. Even going as far as to say, "Something told me," when we know that *something* was the Holy Spirit. The disrespect is bananas. Still, He's ever present, He never changes, the rock-solid foundation to our everyday lives. Unfortunately, some of us have gotten great at ignoring or dismissing the Holy Spirit. A few years ago, I heard a sermon and realized I was quenching the Holy Spirit. 1 Thessalonians 5:19 never made any sense to me until The Holy Spirit uncovered my eyes and allowed me to see the pain it brought Him to be dismissed from the very thing He was brought to do. Jesus told us in John 16:7, "Nevertheless I tell you the truth. It is to your advantage that I go away; for if I do not go away, the Helper will not come to you; but if I depart, I will send Him to you" (NKJV). By quenching Him or not asking for His help, we are stifling His movements in and through us to be able to do what Jesus describes in the next verse in John 16:8, "And when He has come, He will convict the world of sin, and of righteousness, and of judgment" (NKJV). With all that being said, let's consider this, when we ask for the Holy Spirit's help, it cannot be half-hearted. We cannot ask Him and then silence or ignore Him when He begins to pull our card in ways we don't agree with. Two instances I just knew I blew it with the Holy Spirit, but in His grace, He forgave me:

First: I asked the Holy Spirit to prepare me for my Earthly husband. Straight out the gate, I mean before the request left my lips, He said, "You interrupt me all the time. I can't even get the first sentence out without you predicting what I'll say and interjecting. Sometimes, I'll say something and mid-thought, you'll pick up your phone and start scrolling or texting. Or sometimes even as we're talking, you'll use that as a time to get chores done. If you interrupt me like this, you'll do it to your Earthly bridegroom and he won't appreciate it." Jaw on the floor. The best awareness is self-awareness and I had none. I was completely oblivious to this trait, and I began to intentionally correct my faux pas. If you interrupt a person long enough, they might shut down and stop talking. I'm grateful the Holy Spirit didn't shut down on me; instead, He corrected me in love.

SN: Ask the Holy Spirit to help prepare you for your future spouse. He knows the man or woman you are to marry and He knows exactly how to prepare you for them, specifically. If you are already married, ask the Holy Spirit how to love your spouse as they evolve.

Second: He had been talking to me about the seven deadly sins, specifically, gluttony. I told Him I would be more cognizant to honor my hunger cues, but that I needed help. He began to convict me as I ate, but because it had been my pattern since I can remember to overeat, this sin got rebellious. I was eating breakfast and I heard Him say, "The next bite is your last bite." What did I do? Ate two more bites. I know, I know. Please refer to John 8:7 before you judge me. Anyway, as I ignored Him and listened to the god of my stomach, I was carnally satisfied, but my spirit felt guilty. Later, I went to pray and speak with Him, and I could feel Him blatantly ignoring me. It truly felt like my best friend wasn't speaking to me. Finally, I heard Him say, "How is it you can ignore me, but I can't ignore you?" **Grabs chest and falls to knees in spiritual anguish** Okay, maybe that's dramatic, but I felt so bad. This is when I realized there were consequences to quenching The Holy Spirit. This also helped me to realize there are some people that have a seared conscience, and the Holy Spirit has been extinguished. Their convictions are non-existent and their moral compasses are in operation one, maybe two, times a day, whereas a spiritual compass is only possible with the help of the Holy Spirit.

Let these two experiences serve as a lesson, The Holy Spirit has a personality just like the rest of us. He has natural and supernatural character traits that make Him necessary for a believer's walk. The Holy Spirit is an advocate (John 14:25-26). The Holy Spirit is a gift (Acts 2:28). He is power (Acts 1:18). He is our intercessor (Romans 8:26). The Holy Spirit is sacred (Matthew 12:31-32). He has fruit (Galatians 5:22-23). He is our greatest help and the spirit of truth (John 14:16-17). He is a life giver, a way of life, a mindset, and a mind governor (Romans 8:2-6). He is a language giver (Acts 2:1-4) and teaching aid (tutor) (Luke 24:45-47). He is liberty (2 Corinthians 3:17-18). He is the one who seals and guarantees (Ephesians 1:11-14). He is the keeper of our temples (1 Corinthians 6:19-20). The Holy Spirit is the one who convicts, and He is our helper (John 16:7-15). These scriptures are proof He will help us keep and obey God's commandments.

God Help Us to Keep Your Commandments

God, thank you for the commandments you have given us. Even in our gratitude, thanks will never be enough to acknowledge your everlasting kindness. Who are we that you are mindful of us? Thank you for being so kind to our ancestors back in the wilderness that you gave them parameters in the form of commandments. Father, forgive them for the ways in which they disregarded your commandments and forgive us for the ways in which we read what they did to you, yet choose to do the same. God help us to love you in your love language. Help us to love you with the evidence of keeping your commandments. God, you were so intentional to use the word "Keep" in John 14:15; keep often translates as: to guard, to observe, and to attend to carefully. Holy Spirit, help us to guard, observe and attend to your commandments. Holy Spirit, we know how to do nothing with the absence of you, yet we try often. Keeper of our temples, help us to guard God's commandments. Help us to love Him the way He deserves. Show us how to lay down the idol of self and to put the true King on the throne of our hearts. This we ask in Jesus' name, amen!

In what ways have you created an idol of self? List the ways and for each way you've created an idol of self, create a prayer asking God to destroy that idol of self.

Example: You lie to save face.

"God, help me to be honest even if it means I am punished because of my actions, in Jesus' name, amen."

Idolatry of People

*"For do I now persuade men, or God? Or do I seek to please men?
For if I still pleased men, I would not be a bondservant of Christ."*
Galatians 1:10 (NKJV)

What Is Idolatry of People

In a world full of idol worship, naturally an idolatry of people is bound to happen. Along with the worship of deities, the worship of people is very much a crisis in the world and in the body of Christ. Idolatry of people can best be described as choosing or letting the voice of people or a person be louder than the voice of God in your life. An example of this: God told you to move or quit your job. Before you can be obedient to God, you must let your family or friends approve this decision. This is not to be confused with obtaining wise counsel concerning your plans (Proverbs 11:14). Or being submitted to someone further in the faith that will give Godly advice and always point you back to the voice of God. This type of idolatry is when you cannot move to the left or to the right without their approval and their approval usually opposes the voice of God's direction. The idolatry is present because of your deafened discernment, oblivious to the true color of their heart towards you and ultimately towards God. They impart lies into your mind, blaming your spiritual immaturity as a reason why you cannot trust the voice of God on the inside of you. This is manipulation, in addition you could be being controlled under the title, "spiritual son or daughter or spiritual mentee."

I always wanted a spiritual father and/or mother. At the very least, a spiritual mentor, but I never got one, even after begging God for one, it never happened. It seemed like every one of my friends in college had a mentor, but me. It wasn't until recently when I felt like I was coming into a relationship with a spiritual/ business mentor that God told me this, "I couldn't give you a mentor back then because you would have made them an idol. You would have made them your god all while asking me to bless it. A good mentor would have ushered you back to me in every way and refused to let you make them an idol, but by virtue of your idolatry, you would have attracted a mentor that your idol worshiped deserved, one that took advantage of your time, talents and treasure. One that stifled your growth all while tearing down the pieces of security I have built for you. More than likely narcissistic tendencies with a Jezebel and Leviathan spirit. They would have controlled everything you did to prevent your destiny from outshining theirs. I would have told you to make your big move after college and they would have told you the complete opposite, and because of your idol worship to them, you would have listened and not moved; thinking you misheard me." What could I say to this? Everything God spoke to me was true. I would have worshipped the ground this person walked on, and my heart would have grown far from God. These past few years Holy Spirit has been the greatest spiritual mentor and when the time is right, if it be God's will, He will allow my path to cross with someone that can help cultivate the things God has placed on the inside of me.

The best example of this is celebrity culture. Celebrity culture is an unrealistic and unhealthy obsession with celebrities or people of higher influence and status. This culture has also bled into churches. Churches will have an entire section dedicated to those who are deemed celebrities. Before you interject the "honor" argument, save it. All parties in this situation are in error; the church leadership that has sectioned them off to an island where they can be ogled. The "celebrity" for attempting to lay hold of glory present at the church that should be reserved for God. Finally, the consumers and contributors to celebrity culture that won't allow people with influence peace to sit amongst them without being bothered or made to feel uncomfortable.

Examples in The Bible of People Pleasing

There are so many examples in the Bible of idolatry of people.

<u>Let's start with Aaron:</u>

"When the people saw how long it was taking Moses to come back down the mountain, they gathered around Aaron. 'Come on,' they said, 'make us some gods who can lead us. We don't know what happened to this fellow Moses, who brought us here from the land of Egypt.' So Aaron said, 'Take the gold rings from the ears of your wives and sons and daughters, and bring them to me.' All the people took the gold rings from their ears and brought them to Aaron. Then Aaron took the gold, melted it down, and molded it into the shape of a calf. When the people saw it, they exclaimed, 'O Israel, these are the gods who brought you out of the land of Egypt!' Aaron saw how excited the people were, so he built an altar in front of the calf. Then he announced, 'Tomorrow will be a festival to the Lord!'" Exodus 32:1-5 (NLT)

My biggest problem with Aaron is that he knew better. He was God's spokesperson; he was with Moses shooting in the gym (asking Pharoah to let God's people go). Based on the Biblical evidence, Aaron couldn't have lacked that much faith that he thought God abandoned them. This tells us his allegiance to people liking him was greater than his allegiance to God.

<u>Next, Poncious Pilate:</u>

"From then on Pilate sought to release Him, but the Jews cried out, saying, 'If you let this Man go, you are not Caesar's friend. Whoever makes himself a king speaks against Caesar.' Then he delivered Him to them to be crucified. So they took Jesus and led Him away." John 19:12 & 16 (NKJV)

Deep, Heavy Sigh

My God, where's the backbone, but what did we expect? I can't help but notice the similarities in most politicians today. Willing to do anything for the people because they are bought and sold by the people. This was all written and destined to happen–I just hate that Pilate had to go down in history as a hater.

<u>Next, Asa:</u>

"And in the thirty-ninth year of his reign, Asa became diseased in his feet, and his malady was severe; yet in his disease he did not seek the Lord, but the physicians." 2 Chronicles 16:12 (NKJV)

Being in Christ, I've learned that if we are to love Him like we confess we do, we must love every phase, every character, every trait of Him. Asa was blatantly ignoring God the healer, Jehovah Rapha. Asa, like so many of us, put his trust in doctors. He put his trust in the resource and not the source. Why do we look to pills before we ask God to take away that headache or back pain? Why have we bowed down our knees to cancer when God clearly tells us that everything will bow at the name of Jesus (Philippians 2:10–11), that *includes* cancer. That includes the oncologist report; ultimately, whose report will you believe (Isaiah 51:3)?

<u>Next, Saul:</u>

"The men of Israel saw what a tight spot they were in; and because they were hard pressed by the enemy, they tried to hide in caves, thickets, rocks, holes, and cisterns. Some of them crossed the

Jordan River and escaped into the land of Gad and Gilead. Meanwhile, Saul stayed at Gilgal, and his men were trembling with fear. Saul waited there seven days for Samuel, as Samuel had instructed him earlier, but Samuel still didn't come. Saul realized that his troops were rapidly slipping away. So he demanded, 'Bring me the burnt offering and the peace offerings!' And Saul sacrificed the burnt offering himself. Just as Saul was finishing with the burnt offering, Samuel arrived. Saul went out to meet and welcome him, but Samuel said, 'What is this you have done?' Saul replied, 'I saw my men scattering from me, and you didn't arrive when you said you would, and the Philistines are at Micmash ready for battle. So I said, 'The Philistines are ready to march against us at Gilgal, and I haven't even asked for the Lord's help!' So I felt compelled to offer the burnt offering myself before you came.' 'How foolish!' Samuel exclaimed. 'You have not kept the command the Lord your God gave you. Had you kept it, the Lord would have established your kingdom over Israel forever. But now your kingdom must end, for the Lord has sought out a man after his own heart. The Lord has already appointed him to be the leader of his people, because you have not kept the Lord's command.'" 1 Samuel 13:6-14 (NLT)

This is one of my favorite prophetic warnings, "If only you had waited, if only you had obeyed, God would have established your kingdom over Israel forever." Saul compromised a promise for his entire bloodline because of what? His idolatry of man. Verse 11 says, "I saw my men scattering from me..." In the Hebrew, "to scatter" means to shatter, break, dash, to pieces, sunder. Sunder which comes from the same verb as "asunder" in the verse, *"So that they are no more two, but one flesh. What therefore God hath joined together, let not man put asunder." Matthew 19:6 (ASV).* This shows us the root of what might have triggered Saul's hasty decision to disobey God's commandment and unknowingly forfeit his promise. Saul's desire to please people before His God comes from a root of abandonment issues and not wanting people to leave him or to separate from him. I'm sure with more biblical research we could see why this was his case, nonetheless the root has been identified. In the spirit of deliverance, I would encourage Saul to count this trigger as a blessing for highlighting the root that was actually present and lying dormant. I would then encourage him to take an ax to the root of his abandonment issues as he asks God to destroy the fruit (people-pleasing) that the seeds or root of abandonment has rendered. Since Saul is no longer in the land of the living, if you resonated with any of his story, I would encourage you to take an ax to the root of your abandonment issues. It might be too late for him, but not for you.

Next: <u>The Old Prophet vs New Prophet</u>

"Then the king answered and said to the man of God, 'Please entreat the favor of the Lord your God, and pray for me, that my hand may be restored to me.' So the man of God entreated the Lord, and the king's hand was restored to him, and became as before. Then the king said to the man of God, 'Come home with me and refresh yourself, and I will give you a reward.' But the man of God said to the king, 'If you were to give me half your house, I would not go in with you; nor would I eat bread nor drink water in this place. For so it was commanded me by the word of the Lord, saying, 'You shall not eat bread, nor drink water, nor return by the same way you came.'"" 1 Kings 13:6-9 (NKJV)

"...and went after the man of God, and found him sitting under an oak. Then he said to him, 'Are you the man of God who came from Judah?' And he said, 'I am.' Then he said to him, 'Come home with me and eat bread.' And he said, 'I cannot return with you nor go in with you; neither can I eat bread nor drink water with you in this place. For I have been told by the word of the Lord, 'You shall not eat bread nor drink water there, nor return by going the way you came.'" He said to him, 'I too am a prophet as you

are, and an angel spoke to me by the word of the Lord, saying, 'Bring him back with you to your house, so that he may eat bread and drink water.'' (He was lying to him.) *So he went back with him, and ate bread in his house, and drank water." 1 Kings 13:14-19 (NKJV)*

See 1 Kings 13 for a greater context.

Even though it was the old prophet that lied here, God took and un-alived the one who *knew* Him, the one who should have known better. The old prophet was already compromised because he continued to live in Bethel, where a golden calf was set up by Jeroboam, king of Israel (See 1 King 12:28-31). God had to send a prophet from Judah to condemn Jeroboam; however, it's interesting that the young prophet went to go and condemn idol worship yet ended up being an idol worshiper. I have so many questions. Why did the man of God vehemently say no to the king's invitation, but not the old prophet's? Was he hungry and delirious from his journey? Was it an idol of titles and as soon as he heard the old man was a prophet, he immediately felt he could trust him?

SN: This is a lot of Christians, as soon as a man or woman of God's name is preceded by a title, you lose all your discernment and biblical knowledge. In addition, you have those people that must be identified by their title even while they're not in ministry. Why are you making the people at the coffee shop write Prophet so and so on your latte, please simmer down. Is it absolutely necessary that your Facebook name begins with Bishop this or Deacon that? I digress. If it wasn't the title that made him disobey God, what was it? More important than answering this question for the masses, I think it might be essential to personally seek Holy Spirit concerning this matter. Asking Him a few things: Why the young prophet disobeyed God but also ask Him to reveal the state of your heart if you were ever in a situation like this. Have you ever been in a situation like this, what did you do? Sit under the shaded tree of this young prophet for a moment and reflect on what you would have done and why. For those of you already thinking of a shallow answer, keep it. You've made it this far into the book because you have committed some type of idolatry against God. Be real with yourself and Holy Spirit. Please note* It's okay to answer this question from a broken and compromised place. After you've answered it from that region, move to the Goshen of healing and settle there.

A Contrast. Samuel and Eli

"Then the Lord said to Samuel: "Behold, I will do something in Israel at which both ears of everyone who hears it will tingle. On that day I will perform against Eli all that I have spoken concerning his house, from beginning to end. For I have told him that I will judge his house forever for the iniquity which he knows, because his sons made themselves vile, and he did not restrain them. And therefore, I have sworn to the house of Eli that the iniquity of Eli's house shall not be atoned for by sacrifice or offering forever." So Samuel lay down until morning and opened the doors of the house of the Lord. And Samuel was afraid to tell Eli the vision. Then Eli called Samuel and said, "Samuel, my son!" He answered, "Here I am." And he said, "What is the word that the Lord spoke to you? Please do not hide it from me. God do so to you, and more also, if you hide anything from me of all the things that He said to you." Then Samuel told him everything, and hid nothing from him. And he said, "It is the Lord. Let Him do what seems good to Him.""" I Samuel 3:11-18 (NKJV)

Samuel was faced with a difficult burden to shoulder at such a young age. God gave him a word and Samuel had to speak that word out against the man who helped to rear him up. Samuel honored his mentor, Eli, but when it was time, he shifted and declared his allegiance to God as he spoke what thus saith the Lord, even at the expense of his relationship. We don't see people with the character of Samuel very often. Even at a young age, Samuel was set on choosing God before any man.

A Prayer to End People Pleasing:

God, I am a sinner. I am well aware of my sinful ways, yet you love me–thank you. I ask you to forgive me for desiring to please people more than I desire to please you. God, I'm now aware this came from a root of abandonment and/or other traumatic wounds. God, I can no longer live in trauma. I only want to please you. Forgive me for my worship to people, when I should have only worshipped you. Let Heaven and Earth record that this day, I renounce and come out of agreement with my idolatry of people. I dethrone every man or woman off the seat of my heart. Jehovah Sabaoth, I ask you to come and take your rightful place as King and as Lord. I give you rule, reign and dominion in all areas of my life, especially my desire to please people. Whether you do a quick work in my heart or if this is a process of making daily decisions to keep you above all others, I ask the Holy Spirit that you walk with me as I make these decisions. I am a sinner who, like Aaron, would choose the voices of others above your commandment. But today, I have renounced that pattern of thinking and that way of life. Reprogram my mind and my body to only have a Godly loyalty to you–God, rewrite my DNA. Take the desires out of my heart and every other system and cell in my body to place a person's desire above yours. Because you are a good God, I count this done and I seal this deliverance prayer from people-pleasing with the blood of Jesus Christ, amen.

Examples in Real Life

Definition: Idolatry is the worship of someone or something other than God-the father, the son and the Holy Ghost as though it/they were God. Idolatry can also be described as anything you love more than your obedience to God.

Loyalty vs Idolatry

Loyalty-a strong feeling of support or allegiance

Loyalty and idolatry are completely separate. That is until your loyalty for someone causes you to worship that person in place of God. It's okay to "be down" for someone. Our girl Brandy taught us that, but where is the line? Where is the balance? Being loyal to someone should not compromise your loyalty to God. As soon as it does, loyalty idolatry enters the chat.

There was one time a friend of mine hypothetically asked if I would lie to her husband about her whereabouts if she was ever doing something she had no business doing. I immediately told her no and explained my reasoning. In short, if I lied for her, it meant I would deny my allegiance and righteousness in front of God to be loyal to her sinful ways. She eventually understood my point of view. Fast-forward, about a year later, another friend told me, "If my husband calls you, can you tell him xyz (a lie)?" Apprehensively, I said, "Yes." Reasoning, it was important I lie for the greater good. He called. I lied. The conviction of the Lord sat at the bottom of my stomach like some bad chili. That's when the Lord began to deal with me about what I would later realize to be loyalty idolatry. My loyalty or allegiance to my friend encouraged me to compromise my right standing with God, breaking a few of his commandments and precepts. There are so many people in our life we might feel like we, "owe". God freed me in this area as He made me a business owner. When customers purchased books or anything I was selling, I would feel so indebted to them. God began to ask me questions as I explored my feeling of debt to customers, friends and family members. I won't go into detail, but some recurring themes were feelings of inadequacy, worthlessness, and past rejection. With those themes to chew on, I ask you, "Why do you feel like you owe this person/people" Why do you feel like you owe this person/people more allegiance than your God?" The same God that sent His only son to die so you could live. The same God that sent His son to die a horrible death so you wouldn't have to. Take your time to answer. Dig deep and be released from the debt of people like God released me.

Honor vs Idolatry

Honor-regard with great respect or esteem.

Like the story of the young prophet and the old prophet in 1 Kings 13, who are you honoring when there is no honor due? Multiple times throughout the Bible, God tells His people, namely, His prophet Jeremiah not to pray for people because of their heart (Jeremiah 7:16 & Jeremiah 11:14). He told Samuel to stop mourning or keeping his honor with Saul once God had located another, a man after His own heart. In the Message Bible, at the end of Amos 9:1-4 it explains how because of their blatant sin, God had made up His mind to hurt them and not to help them. Too often people we deem "Honorable" have fallen from honor in the sight of God, yet we make them our "god's" and give them what God has stopped giving. Why? I'll answer that for you. Your honor has turned into idolatry. You are more obedient to respecting this person more than you are God. You would rather argue and/or ignore the Holy Spirit's command about this person or group of people. Here's the good news: You can repent, renounce your misplaced honor and be delivered through knowledge, today! Here's the bad news: Should you decide to continue in honoring someone who like Saul, God's favor and spirit has left, you'll be in good company with those angels that decided to follow Lucifer down to Earth as he was thrown out of Heaven like a streak of lightning (See Revelations 12). Let Heaven and Earth witness, this day, God has set before you life and death, blessing and cursing... choose life! (Deuteronomy 30:19).

Root of Idolatry of People

To every fruit is a seed that was planted and watered knowingly or unknowingly. Generally, people pleasing starts during childhood. Wanting to please emotionally unstable or double-minded adults around you. Having to always think three steps ahead of them to remain safe. Compensating for the lack of control by being whatever anyone needed you to be, or feeling so rejected, you vow to be everything to anyone in order to feel worthy of love. Another possible entry point of people pleasing if you were blessed with a somewhat big "T" trauma free childhood, is in adolescence or adulthood when you were extremely vulnerable-emotionally, mentally, physically, and/ or spiritually. While there is a gamut of entry points, the last one I'd like to submit is via your bloodline. Your mom could never say "no" and you can't either. Your dad is always trying to make everyone happy, at the expense of himself and you do the same. It's a learned behavior and now you've followed in their footsteps. The bloodline iniquity worker knows pleasing people won't only run you into the ground like it did those in previous generations, but it will also be a blockade between you and God. And God, being holy won't compete with your whorish desire to make and please other gods before Him, thus the start or continuation of the great divide. The only fate for this lifestyle are those ear throbbing words from Matthew 7:23 (KJV) "And then will I profess unto them, I never knew you: depart from me, ye that work iniquity."

Take a few moments to do some reflection: When do you think people-pleasing entered your life?

Ask Holy Spirit to bring back to memory those moments in which your allegiance from God was stolen. Call back those pieces of your fragmented soul. Decree and declare this as often as you deem necessary: "I am not a people-pleaser, I don't need validation from people, only from God." Please note You can also do* *this on behalf of your bloodline according to Leviticus 26:40-46, Isaiah 58:12 and Ezekiel 22:30. However, this kind does not go out except by prayer and fasting" Matthew 17:21. The Greek word for kind translates to genos, meaning, "kindred, offspring, stock, tribe, nation, family, etc." Some bloodline iniquities are so stubborn they will only respond to killing your flesh, turning down your plate and fasting. They have had the legal right for thousands of years to molest your bloodline and won't even begin to take your prayers seriously until you have done a Biblical definition of a fast (abstain* from all foods and sometimes water for a period of time).

Revelation 12:11

In the last few years, the Lord has had me make YouTube videos on some pretty controversial topics; that really shouldn't be controversial, because if the Bible says it's wrong, our opinions don't matter, but I deviate. I was in heavy prayer before I made them (stalling), but finally I just did it because I felt the Lord growing impatient with my allegiance to what others thought as opposed to His commands. YouTube seemed to upload these videos exceptionally fast that day, the videos were uploaded (*Why the LGBTQIA Slogan Of "Pride" Has A Demonic Agenda* and *Why I Denounced a Greek Sorority),* and a spirit of offense was unleashed. Many of my family members found themselves offended, and few had the courage to tell me to my face why they thought I was wrong. I knew not to argue with them because this wasn't a flesh and blood *(Ephesians 6:12)* matter and I knew reasoning with a spirit of offense *(Proverbs 18:19)* would have been useless. Immediate concern came into my spirit because while I love the thought of being a "Kingdom Disrupter" the actual process of disrupting *is* spiritual warfare. Up until I denounced the sorority, I had never gone against the grain in my bloodline. Everyone is fine when you're a lukewarm Christian, but when you begin rooting up generational curses and destroying evil covenants, the true colors show. As I was hearing the feedback, I began to feel like I was losing the people I loved the most. In those moments, I realized some people proclaim to be Christians yet have views opposite of the Father. As I kept responding, "This is what God has asked me to speak about." I felt my "why" growing weaker. I knew I was the repairer of the breach *(Isaiah 58:12)* and I knew being the blueprint was difficult, but I never expected this. Ignorantly asking God to trust me when I didn't have a reference point of how to be the repairer of the breach, because I had no blueprint. Only to later realize Jesus was my reference point, but in that moment of persecution, I couldn't see beyond my own front door. Feeling like I would be disowned in my own family for my Christ-like views, I begin to weep in the presence of God. Where I thought I would feel a garment of comfort and pity, God met me with a Fatherly warning that gives me chills even as I write this. As tears filled my eyes, He said, *"You came to me and told me you would be a Kingdom disrupter. You told me, you would cry loud and spare not. You asked me for that YouTube platform and when I gave it to you, you promised you would speak only the things I desired. Now, when faced with pushback and contention you toil with the thought of sugarcoating what I have to say as not to be offensive. My very name is offensive to a sinner! So, if you want to be my mouthpiece you have a choice to make. Me or them. If moving forward, I ask you to publicly speak on something contrary to their "beliefs" and in fear of what they would think, you deny me, I will then know that they have become a god in your life. Kayla, I make war with gods. My very name is Jealous. I will cause dissension in the relationships, and you will lose them. I won't compete with your family, and I won't compete with your friends. I am the first and final authority–what I say goes. He who loves his father or mother more than Me is not worthy of Me (Matthew 10:37).* You set your face like a flint and speak only what the spirit of truth would have you say and then you close your mouth. "Who is he who speaks and it comes to pass,

When the Lord has not commanded it?" *Lamentations 3:37 (NKJV)*. If I ask you to do something and someone in your life tells you to do something different, they have now become an enemy to *me* in *your* life. Whoa unto them that falls into the hands of a living God."

I have never been read this hard by God–In. My. Life. Towards me, I've only known Him as God the Lamb. This day, the lion showed His teeth, and the fear of God was engrafted in my heart. As the fear of the Lord grew, the fear of man decreased. That day Jeremiah 1:17 became my motto "Get yourself ready! Stand up and say to them whatever I command you. Do not be terrified by them, or I will terrify you before them" (NIV). The idolatry and desire to please people still arises from time to time, then I remember the warning of the Lord. I would hate to lose someone in my life because I have made their opinion of me a god. I'm not perfect, but I press towards the mark.

Some Additional Signs You Might Have an Idol of People:

- Needing the approval of everyone.

- Trust in people more than God.

- Thinking people are your source, when they are only a resource.

- Asking the opinions of others before consulting Holy Spirit.

- You believe in people (doctors) to heal you more than God.

- Idolatry in politics, culture, etc...

- Compromising one's body and/or morals to keep a relationship.

- You care deeply about what people think, e.g. someone who won't leave their sorority or fraternity because of what people think.

Prophetic Word Idolatry

You might see this subtitle and think, *okay now she's just making ways to be idolatrous.* I swear this is a thing connected to an even bigger *thing.* Idolatry of prophetic words is a fruit of idolatry of people. Keep in mind, idolatry of people produces much fruit, sour fruit, but still fruit. This type of idolatry comes from a place of real need, extreme deficit. You want to be seen, you want someone, anyone to come to you and tell you just how amazing you are or to speak into a future God has already created. We do this with people, with things (magic 8 ball), horoscopes, and even artificial intelligence (AI). While idolatry sometimes can pervert prophecy, please don't misunderstand the significance of the office of a prophet, the gift of prophecy, and flowing in the spirit of prophecy. The office of a prophet is held for those called from birth, they are called to: direct, correct, warn, govern, and equip. Plainly put in Jeremiah 1:10, "See, I have this day set you over the nations and over the kingdoms, To root out and to pull down, To destroy and to throw down, To build and to plant" (NKJV). The gift of prophecy is for edification, exhortation, and comfort to the body of Christ *(See 1 Corinthians 14).* Finally, the spirit of prophecy, empowers the body of Christ for ministry of reconciliation *(Revelation 19:10 & 2 Corinthians 5:18-19).* All three are essential to the body of Christ and there is countless scripture to confirm this. The problem I want to highlight is when individuals look to these three ways as the only source of God speaking, as a result, skipping time in God's presence growing deeper in intimacy. He is the source, everyone else is the resource. It's like the game "Telephone." The first person starts with a statement, as the statement travels around the circle through whispers, the statement begins to lose its structure. Finally, the last person intended to declare what was to be spoken aloud, repeat something completely different than what was originally spoken. That's what we settle for when we would prefer a word from someone else other than God. Yes, there are prophets that hear straight from the heart of God and are extremely accurate, but as fate would have it, our idolatry *will* attract prophets who, just like the last person in the game of Telephone, will be loud and wrong. Here's what the Bible says about it:

""Son of man, these leaders have set up idols in their hearts. They have embraced things that will make them fall into sin. Why should I listen to their requests? Tell them, 'This is what the Sovereign Lord says: The people of Israel have set up idols in their hearts and fallen into sin, and then they go to a prophet asking for a message. So I, the Lord, will give them the kind of answer their great idolatry deserves. I will do this to capture the minds and hearts of all my people who have turned from me to worship their detestable idols.'" Ezekiel 14:3-5 (NLT)

When you're feeling this way, take those desires to God. *God, I'm feeling like I need validation, I'm feeling like I want someone to come and tell me how amazing I am, tell me the plans you have for me.* That's when He might lead you to Jeremiah 29:11 or Deuteronomy 28:13; reminding you, you're a King's Kid! Through me, the Holy Spirit wrote a book of Biblical affirmations for children called *Hey King's Kid* and it not only helped to restore the validation and exhortations I needed as a child, but it's helping thousands of children be affirmed in God. As I was penning this book, pieces of my inner child began to mend after so long of being broken. I can't speak on anything I haven't lived out. There was a season I wanted prophetic words more than God, but it seemed like every prophet, apostle and donkey would skip over me. While this caused more rejection, it also pushed me back into the arms of the Father for answers I thought men and mere creation could give me. I sought the

LORD, and He answered me; He delivered me from all my fears. When I looked to Him, I became radiant with joy; because of this, my face will never be ashamed. *(Psalms 34:4-5).* As I sought Him, I realized He was desiring to minister personal prophetic words to me. The unfortunate part was that because of my idolatry, I didn't see those words as poignant. I had become so desensitized to God speaking to me that I didn't even realize how profound the master's words were. I needed everyone to confirm what God wanted to do personally as He spoke to me and what God wanted to do. As Ezekiel 14 stated, I was destined to get a confirmation or an answer my idolatry deserved. In God's judgment of my heart posture, He allowed the devil into my mind with deceptive tactics. Not realizing the devil also gives confirmations. Idolatry opened the door for deception to speak louder than any other voice of reason. God is a gentleman as much as it grieves His heart, He will step out of the way so you can cheat on Him with your sin and your god.

Something to reflect on:

Maybe it's not prophetic words that you worship, but you cannot make a decision unless 49 people co-sign or unless your mom and best friend encourage you to do so. Maintaining your own identity in Christ, but at the drop of a hat, willing to forsake Christ at your family, friend or partner's command. Why is it that their voice means more to you than God's?

Revelation 12:11

After I had broken up with someone I really cared about, God began to show me the idolatry I had was no longer towards this person, but towards marriage. God told me He was healing me. I fasted, prayed and submitted to His process, but the healing wasn't coming fast enough. I was still in pain and bitterness seemed to be chasing me down faster than I could run. I saw there was a healing and deliverance service put on by an Apostle who was in town. I "prayed" about it, but in my heart, my mind was already made up *(Isaiah 30:2-3)*. I invited a friend because idolatry always invites others to join in its wickedness. Not realizing this apostle was a wolf in sheep's clothing, I hoop and holler during his sermon due to my lack of sharp discernment and go up for the altar call. Thank God for the two cents I still had. I ask God to make me and my friend impenetrable to any evil impartations in case he was really a false teacher. This "apostle" skipped right by my friend and only later to find out she was praying, "God if this man is a false apostle, allow him to skip over me." I wish somebody would have told me to pray that, although I wonder if it would have worked because of my idolatry of looking for my healing in a human source. Nonetheless, he comes to me and begins to ask questions. Very on brand for what a familiar spirit might do. He doesn't say it, but spiritually, I see he's unable to get a "reading" on me, so he gets frustrated and turns to his armor bearers. He was laughing and taunting me, accusing me of, "Not wanting to be delivered." This man proceeds to hit me on top of my head multiple times saying, "Come out, come out of her." At this point, I'm shaking because a man has never put their hands on me. He asks the "thugs" with him to pull me back to him as I back away, trying to dodge his hits. Finally, in frustration, he walks off and asks a woman to pray for me before I can go back to my seat. I go back to my seat utterly confused and sore, asking God what just happened. I'm ready to go because at this point, this man is an abuser, not a minister. My friend is still at the altar; while I wait for her at the exit, I hear God say a couple of things: *1. Why did you think that man could heal you better than I could? 2. This could have gone a whole lot worse, but you asked me to make you impenetrable. 3. You thought someone could lay hands on you and miraculously heal you, but the devil uses agents to lay hands as well. 4. Do you know the level of spirits you could be taking home because of your idolatry of people? Heavier spirits than the sadness you're feeling now could have jumped all over you because of your presence in their territory.* After putting my friend and I in physical and spiritual danger, I realized I was trusting in chariots and horses *(Psalms 20:7)* when I should have been trusting in God. I go into a deep repentance and decide to *fully* submit and trust God on my healing journey. Not even a month later, the gray skies began to turn blue again. Sometimes we dread God's way because we think we can microwave something faster, but cooked food always tastes better and lasts longer than microwaved food.

Idolatry of Politics

As elections take place every one year, two years, and four years, the masses act as if we lack the sense common to man. We get behind politicians as if they are paying our electricity bill. Showing God that our obedience is to a specific side and not to Jesus Christ *(Isaiah 9:6)*. I'm not here to condemn us–just to ask that we take a few things into consideration:

- Maybe the candidate you want to vote for does *know* the Lord, but even Satan knows and acknowledges God. Does it reflect in their policies?

- There's Christ, then there is culture. Christ and culture will always conflict.

- Are you voting the same way your family has always voted or are you voting the way God told you to vote?

- Are you voting based on that person's skin color, economic, or cultural background? In the Kingdom of God, there's only one race.

As the next election in your city, state, and nation occurs, don't be led by your emotions or your heart. Ask God who He wants in office to push His Kingdom agenda forward. All throughout 1st and 2nd Kings, with every compromised ruler, it pushed the Children of Israel further from God. That candidate is a city council leader today, but president tomorrow; and with the same demonic agenda that your lack of discernment voted them in with. Every election counts. Be led by the spirit with every ballot you cast.

Idolatry of Race

God gave us a gift of the rainbow embedded within our skin, and we have turned His gift into a weapon. We have turned His gift into hate. Ultimately, we have turned His gift into a basis for war. What started off during those six days of creation as one race, the human race, has manifested into "us against them" because of sin. Countless wars and riots were fought because one race thought they were better than the next.

I don't want to dismiss the pain minorities have felt from those who consider themselves superior, thus deciding to enslave whom they consider less than. I do, however, want us to consider that some minorities have built systems, businesses, organizations on the foundation of their hate of another race. Even while doing inspirational things for their race, the nucleus of the system is racial hate of another. Two wrongs don't make a right. What was supposed to empower shifted into a mindset and essentially a complex. The very same complex that devised the hate in the beginning.

Indications you have made your skin color an idol:

- You don't date outside of your race.

- You adopt polarizing mindsets that divide based on race.

- Avoiding an area, city, state, country due to the race of people that occupy the space. (Disclaimer: Please use wisdom when discerning this as an indication for you personally. Some places should be avoided as some areas are legitimately dangerous for certain people.)

- Adopting mindsets and stereotypes about a specific race.

- You have a hard time choosing between God and your race. E.g. you're Black, White, Hispanic, Asian, etc. before you're a child of God.

- You love your country more than your obedience to God.

Say it with me, *I pledge allegiance to the God of the Holy Bible, amen.*

Warning Against Idolatry of People

This chapter would be incomplete and lacking if I didn't at least mention the reward for your idolatry of people. Scripture will do far more than my words could ever; enjoy!

<u>Reward: a thing given in recognition of one's service, effort, or achievement</u>

"The sorrows [pain and suffering] of those who have chosen another god will be multiplied [because of their idolatry]; I will not pour out their drink offerings of blood, Nor will I take their names upon my lips." Psalms 16:4 (AMP)

"Those who regard worthless idols Forsake their own Mercy."

Jonah 2:8 (NKJV)

"Now the works of the flesh are evident, which are: adultery, fornication, uncleanness, lewdness, idolatry, sorcery, hatred, contentions, jealousies, outbursts of wrath, selfish ambitions, dissensions, heresies, envy, murders, drunkenness, revelries, and the like; of which I tell you beforehand, just as I also told you in time past, that those who practice such things will not inherit the kingdom of God." Galatians 5:19-21 (NKJV)

"Then the people of Judah and Jerusalem will pray to their idols and burn incense before them. But the idols will not save them when disaster strikes!" Jeremiah 11:12 (NLT)

"Get yourself ready! Stand up and say to them whatever I command you. Do not be terrified by them, or I will terrify you before them." Jeremiah 1:17 (NIV)

"Go and cry out to the gods you have chosen. Let them save you when you are in trouble!" Judges 10:14 (NIV)

""Cursed is anyone who makes an idol—a thing detestable to the Lord, the work of skilled hands—and sets it up in secret." Then all the people shall say, "Amen!"" Deuteronomy 27:15 (NIV)

"...and changed the glory of the incorruptible God into an image made like corruptible man—and birds and four-footed animals and creeping things. Therefore God also gave them up to uncleanness, in the lusts of their hearts, to dishonor their bodies among themselves, who exchanged the truth of God for the lie, and worshiped and served the creature rather than the Creator, who is blessed forever. Amen. And even as they did not like to retain God in their knowledge, God gave them over to a debased mind, to do those things which are not fitting;" Romans 1:23-25, 28 (NKJV)

"The children gather wood, the fathers kindle the fire, and the women knead dough, to make cakes for the queen of heaven; and they pour out drink offerings to other gods, that they may provoke Me to anger." Jeremiah 7:18 (NKJV)

"No one can serve two masters; for either he will hate the one and love the other, or else he will be loyal to the one and despise the other. You cannot serve God and mammon." Matthew 6:24 (NKJV)

"Then it shall be, if you by any means forget the Lord your God, and follow other gods, and serve them and worship them, I testify against you this day that you shall surely perish." Deuteronomy 8:19 (NKJV)

"The coming of the lawless one is according to the working of Satan, with all power, signs, and lying wonders, and with all unrighteous deception among those who perish, because they did not receive the love of the truth, that they might be saved. And for this reason God will send them strong delusion, that they should believe the lie, that they all may be condemned who did not believe the truth but had pleasure in unrighteousness." 2 Thessalonians 2:9-12 (NKJV)

""Son of man, these men have set up their idols in their hearts, and put before them that which causes them to stumble into iniquity. Should I let Myself be inquired of at all by them? "Therefore speak to them, and say to them, 'Thus says the Lord God: "Everyone of the house of Israel who sets up his idols in his heart, and puts before him what causes him to stumble into iniquity, and then comes to the prophet, I the Lord will answer him who comes, according to the multitude of his idols, that I may seize the house of Israel by their heart, because they are all estranged from Me by their idols." '" Ezekiel 14:3-5 (NKJV)

"So will I choose their delusions, And bring their fears on them; Because, when I called, no one answered, When I spoke they did not hear; But they did evil before My eyes, And chose that in which I do not delight."" Isaiah 66:4 (NKJV)

"And even as they did not like to retain God in their knowledge, God gave them over to a reprobate mind, to do those things which are not convenient;" Romans 1:28 (KJV)

Until I came into the revelation about idolatry, I was so wrapped in it I couldn't even spell spiritual fidelity. While I didn't know what it was, nor understand the caliber of damage it was doing to me and my relationship with God, He did provide signs to let me know, "Dead end. Going the wrong way. Exit now. Caution. Yield. Rough road ahead. Wrong way. High crash area." When I joined a new church, he warned me not to make the pastor an idol. Idolatry has been the cause behind some of the most painful situations in my life. Half of the tears collected on my behalf stored in Heaven wouldn't be necessary had it not been for my idolatry. I wish I would have known this, I didn't. God is redeeming my story through my testimony as I warn you.

Recovering From People Pleasing Idolatry

I write this in faith believing you have been delivered through knowledge from the idolatry of people pleasing. As a recovering people pleaser, I welcome you to freedom. Freedom to do and say only what the Lord would have you do. Freedom from having to consider 55 different opinions (including your own). As you bask in this newfound freedom, there's something to remember. Maintenance. When considering the deliverance process, people rarely discuss the maintenance of deliverance. Your soul's salvation must be worked out with fear and trembling *(Philippians 2:12)*. You can be delivered from something one day, but if you go back to or around the same habits, people, things, and/or ways of thinking, your deliverance won't last. The spirits will return to you with even greater vengeance *(Matthew 12:43-45)*. Seek God as you find out the best ways to maintain your deliverance from idolatry of people.

Below, make a plan as to how you will refrain from pleasing people. Here are some ideas, but be led by Holy Spirit:

- Create an affirmation statement about how you're worthy, even if people are not happy with you.

- Decrees and declarations such as: "I am not a people pleaser, I don't need validation from people, only God."

- Find the root of why you feel the need to people please. (E.g. avoiding conflict, attachment issues, fear, rejection, abandonment, upbringing, low-self-esteem, validation, etc.)

As you locate yourself further from pleasing people, you might find that individuals who are still caught in the cycle of pleasing vex you and are worthy of your pity. The idolatrous altar in them will offend the delivered-from-idolatry altar in you. At any rate, have grace for them; yet demand they rise. Share the testimony of your idolatry of people and its almost detrimental ending. Pray and believe for their deliverance too. Only if you feel God-led, walk this deliverance out in community with them.

Pray This Prayer:

God, I come to you as a sinner. I'm not worthy of being in your presence, yet you call me friend. Thank you for rescuing me from the idolatry of people. Thank you for giving me the strength to eradicate every voice that is not like yours out of my life. Thank you for rescuing me. Father, forgive me for allowing the trauma and pain of my past to dictate my future. Forgive me for doing what was "normal" and not what was holy. Thank you that now in my repentance, my sins are as far as the east is from the west. As I walk this journey of being delivered from the idolatry of people, Ebenezer, stone of help, I need you. Help me as I choose you. Help me as I filter the wise counsel that comes from you and the wise counsel that comes from the wisdom of this world. Help me to never turn on you, on your word. I have placed people above you for far too long—no more. Help me to never be codependent on people—only you. Give me strength, God for the journey ahead. Let all the other names, words, and opinions fade away. Amen.

Idolatry of Marriage

"Idolatry is to God, what adultery is to a marriage."

-Tiffany Buckner

The Bible begins and ends with a marriage ceremony. In Genesis 2:22 and Revelation 19:6-9, God proves to us He not only values marriage, but believes it is the alpha and the omega; thus, prioritizes the Biblical institution of it. God shows us marriage is His idea by giving us a perfect example of it when He asked His only son to sacrifice His life as the bride price of His people. A people who God describes in Hosea 1:2 as harlots because of their departure from the Lord. There are many times as a society we have strayed far from God's original intent of marriage, doing what our flesh wills instead of His will. On the conveyor belt of idolatry indoctrination, idolatry of marriage is at the top. This looks like treating or romanticizing the institution of marriage with excessive or even misplaced reverence. Offering a worship and obedience that was only meant for the creator Himself. Whenever there is ignorance for the proper use of a thing, naturally, we lessen the value of the original intent and purpose–no fault to that thing or to its creator. Ironic how sin entered the world through the promise of knowledge yet making us more ignorant beyond words. What if sin had not entered the world? What if the spirit of compromise had not hit Adam and Eve in Genesis? Would the Pergamum Church have gotten a letter in Revelations 2:12-17? What would the institution of marriage look like today had compromise not entered into society?

Let's look at God's original intent for marriage:

Procreate- "Then God blessed them, and God said to them, "Be fruitful and multiply; fill the earth and subdue it; have dominion over the fish of the sea, over the birds of the air, and over every living thing that moves on the earth."" *Genesis 1:28 (NKJV)*

Companionship- "And the Lord God said, "*It is* not good that man should be alone; I will make him a helper comparable to him."" *Genesis 2:18 (NKJV)*

To Push God's Will on the Earth- "'Again I say to you that if two of you agree on earth concerning anything that they ask, it will be done for them by My Father in heaven. For where two or three are gathered together in My name, I am there in the midst of them.'" *Matthew 18:19-20 (NKJV)*

While this was God's purpose for marriage, because we've strayed from God's original intent for marriage, idolatry entered the chat and loudly proclaimed it was okay for a man to decide whether it was good for them to be alone or not. With a fine print that stated the man knew the best spouse to choose (man or woman) and the perfect timing to choose one. Forgetting that God gave us His perfect timeline through His example with Adam. In Genesis 2:15, we see God gave Adam placement and purpose. In Genesis 2:16-17, He gave Adam instruction. In Genesis 2:18, He decided it wasn't good for man to be alone. In Genesis 2:19-20, God formed the animals and gave Adam a task. This is when *Adam* realized there was no helper for him. Adam realized what God already did–that it wasn't good for him to be alone. In Genesis 2:21, God took out the part of Adam that couldn't accompany him to his next season–his marital season. In Genesis 2:22, God took all that He spent doing with Adam in the previous chapters and made Eve, and after, He presented her to her husband. In Genesis 2:23-24, Adam saw himself in Eve and made the decision to make her his wife. In Genesis 2:25, God continued to write and narrate their love story.

Genesis so vividly paints the portrait of a God-designed marriage; of two becoming one. Idolatry flips the natural order, as a result we see this timeline executed out of order or attempted with vital missing pieces. Examples of modern-day idolatry concerning God's order might look like Adam spending no time with God, thus never finding his purpose or placement. This same Adam pursuing Eve or is pursued by Eve while housing an additional rib that does not belong to him. Idolatry makes allowances for a woman not allowing herself to be made over by God and the man not allowing himself to be cut open by God. Completely skipping the preparation process but wondering why "love" always seems to fail. Idolatry also blinds us to the type of helper we need and the type of helper we are called to be. Instead of choosing from a healed place, we choose from one of the many pieces of our fragmented soul. Choosing a helper based on deficits within ourselves; a generation of people that choose spouses based on their trauma. The desire to be loved, disguised as a desire to be married; only fulfilling the loneliness that walks the halls of their soul. God told us in Genesis 2:18 it wasn't good for man to be alone and suddenly His people forgot how to enjoy their own company.

As a result of this idolatry and much more, God was forced to silence the voice of the bride and bridegroom in Jeremiah 16. It wouldn't be until the people repented of their sins that God awakes the voice of the bride and bridegroom in Jeremiah 33. *Read the book of Jeremiah for more context*

"For thus says the Lord of hosts, the God of Israel: "Behold, I will cause to cease from this place, before your eyes and in your days, the voice of mirth and the voice of gladness, the voice of the bridegroom and the voice of the bride. "And it shall be, when you show this people all these words, and they say to you, 'Why has the

Lord pronounced all this great disaster against us? Or what is our iniquity? Or what is our sin that we have committed against the Lord our God?' then you shall say to them, 'Because your fathers have forsaken Me,' says the Lord; 'they have walked after other gods and have served them and worshiped them, and have forsaken Me and not kept My law. And you have done worse than your fathers, for behold, each one follows the dictates of his own evil heart, so that no one listens to Me." Jeremiah 16:9-12 (NKJV)

'"Thus says the Lord: 'Again there shall be heard in this place —of which you say, "It is desolate, without man and without beast"—in the cities of Judah, in the streets of Jerusalem that are desolate, without man and without inhabitant and without beast, the voice of joy and the voice of gladness, the voice of the bridegroom and the voice of the bride, the voice of those who will say: "Praise the Lord of hosts, For the Lord is good, For His mercy endures forever"—and of those who will bring the sacrifice of praise into the house of the Lord . For I will cause the captives of the land to return as at the first,' says the Lord . "Thus says the Lord of hosts: 'In this place which is desolate, without man and without beast, and in all its cities, there shall again be a dwelling place of shepherds causing their flocks to lie down. In the cities of the mountains, in the cities of the lowland, in the cities of the South, in the land of Benjamin, in the places around Jerusalem, and in the cities of Judah, the flocks shall again pass under the hands of him who counts them,' says the Lord . 'Behold, the days are coming,' says the Lord, 'that I will perform that good thing which I have promised to the house of Israel and to the house of Judah:' Jeremiah 33:10-14 (NKJV)

What Idolatry Really Made Me Do

Idolatry tricked me into turning on God. It spoke to me and told me things that were not true about Him. There were many days as I was unknowingly being purged of idolatry that I would have to vow to not turn on my Lord and Savior. I would vow to *Wait Well*. Whereas before, I was known for acting up in front of company (the devil) and not siding with God even though He wasn't the one to blame. I would accuse Him of things that my idolatry of marriage, lust, and people caused. God was so gentle, He took the hits. In return for my abuse of our relationship, God gave me peace when I deserved to be tormented because of the portals I opened to sin. Still being kind enough to make the exchange with me; taking on my spirit of heaviness and accepting my cloak of praise. A broken spirit was a soft reward for what I should have received. God was supportive and so kind to me. As I began to grow and mature, yet still under the scales of deception caused by my idolatry, I had to decide to study God's character. Every part of my flesh looking to be offended with God (Acts 24:16), I pushed past the pain. Daily and sometimes even hourly, as tears mounted my face, I had to whisper to myself, "My God wouldn't hurt me like this. God wouldn't do *this* to me. He's just not cruel,' because the pain I felt was cruel. I had to learn to decipher the enemy's voice from God's. I had to remind myself of the goodness of the Lord. I had to recite His promises during the process of studying the cadence of His voice vs the devil's vs. my own. Feeling crushed and not knowing what sin I committed to deserve the level of suffering with the theme of this season in my life being, "Why do I always have such bad luck with men?" Even now as I travel back to those moments while in the thick of deception and ache, I'm reminded of just how child-like we are. When a child experiences any new level of pain for the first time, it's the worst pain they have ever experienced and they're sure to let everyone around them know as they wail in agony. While the adults in their life are consoling them, reassuring them they'll be okay, the child is unsure because they are at an unknown and new knowledge pain. At this moment their tolerance grows because now they know and are familiar with another level of pain. Some of the worst torment I have ever experienced was from the consequences of idolatry and since then, every level of pain I have known has been because of idolatry. I now know that something was dying in that suffering. When cancer patients go through chemotherapy, in an attempt to kill the cancerous cells, the process can often kill some healthy cells as well. In these moments of idolatry, God knew that to kill idolatry in me, He had to kill off some mindsets, thought processes and generational patterns as well. These weren't necessarily "bad", but they had to die so they couldn't one day morph into enemies against my soul. "Most assuredly, I say to you, unless a grain of wheat falls into the ground and dies, it remains alone; but if it dies, it produces much grain." *John 12:24 (NKJV)*. He had to kill my flesh so He could bring me back to life. A new creation, the old passed away.

Revelation 12:11

In 2016, I felt like I heard the Lord tell me a certain man I knew of from my college campus was my husband. I immediately rejected it, but eventually I got on board. When I got on board, I began to obsess over him. For about five years, he began to totally consume every part of my thoughts. I would dream of the day he would have the revelation to make me his girlfriend. We had no interactions because I heard the Lord say, in addition to telling me that he was my husband, it's He who finds a wife; so, I needed to wait for him to pursue. We would have small interactions every now and again, but nothing serious. I planned every holiday around the possibility of finally being with him. Disappointment after disappointment, because all an idol can ever do is disappoint you. Finally, as I prepared to move after graduation, I anticipated moving to a city near him, that way when he asked to be with me, I would already be close (Please don't judge me, as I recount and write this— I too am cringing). After I fasted and heard from the Lord to move to a different state after graduation, I was confused but confident

God could do anything. I moved almost 1,000 miles away, yet my heart was stuck under this man's shoe. Pining after a man that never would be mine. In December 2020, I felt like I heard the Lord say we would be married this time next year. I put my faith around it by telling my community and beginning to believe. As the months closed in, I grew more devastated, but somehow more grounded in faith, believing what God spoke over must come to pass. December 2021 comes and goes and even in all that, I still believed God to do the impossible. Still believing in my miracle marriage, I visited a new church in May 2022. A prophetic word goes out in the house and the pastor says, "I hear God saying some of you have been experiencing something for five years and God says it's coming to an end." It had been a little over five years since I got the prophetic word about this man being my husband, but I just knew it was for me. I thought God was going to finally make it happen. I never imagined what happened next would be my reality. I had a conference in June, and I felt from the Lord...

I want to pause here: Notice how I keep saying, "I felt, I had a feeling." This is not sustainable–feelings come and go. Oftentimes, we are slaves to our feelings, making them an idol. Not to mention, sometimes the thing we think is God, is really a familiar spirit speaking to us. It's important to know that you know, you heard from God. To test the fruit and to test the spirit of a word (1 John 4:1). Feelings are fleeting.

Resuming now…

I was supposed to see him in June because the city I was traveling to was the state he was living in. As my time in this city came to an end, one night in the hotel room, in the midst of what felt like betrayal from God, a suicidal ideation was submitted to my mind. What I didn't know then, but I know now, is that this idea came from the spirit of deception that had legal rights and an open door because of my idolatry. It had legalities in the spiritual realm to encourage me to take my life. I agreed with that spirit and decided I could no longer take the pain of being "betrayed" by God, so I began to think of the best options to make it happen that night or soon after. During my suicide plans and while almost buried in the sea of my tears, Yeshua, my deliverer, violently and swiftly carried me off to sleep. I woke up the next morning afraid to open my eyes because I couldn't remember the fate I chose for myself the night before. I sat up in bed no longer feeling a spirit of sorrow or suicide. What I didn't know was the idolatry in my life had legal right to present to me a spirit of suicide, but it was the grace of God that I was taken to sleep before I could answer. I saw the sunlight and decided it was time to let the promise go. I packed my bags but chose to leave the biggest bag I carried for five plus years in that city and went home. It's important to mention that in May 2021, I felt an unctioning from the Lord to make a YouTube video in faith declaring to the world that God told me who my husband was *and* that I had full belief He would make it happen. This would be followed by six other short videos giving my subscribers tips on how to date while knowing who their future spouse is, how to stay in faith, who to tell and who not to tell, etc. A few weeks after my hotel events, someone comments on one of my videos and tells me how what I'm believing is not real and that I'm in deception. Another subscriber would make a mini-series on how "someone" she subscribed to on YouTube was living in deception and proceed to send me a video of her talking about me. An immediate spirit of offense grew because I've spent the better part of six months fighting the naysayers in my comments and in my life telling me it wasn't God speaking to me. Not understanding why strangers would go to such lengths to discourage me in this process. Even though the walls of offense were built, these comments had already penetrated a deep place of doubt that led to curiosity, that just maybe I was in deception. I went to what I thought was the voice of God about it, but I couldn't get a clear answer. I knew Him to not be the author of confusion (1 Corinthians 14:33), but at this time my head was spinning. I spent the better part of June and July of 2022 in a frenzy. Towards the end of July, I discovered Stephanie Ike Okafor's sermon on YouTube entitled, "Exposing Deception." I heard from the Lord I was to watch it and not even halfway through I was convicted. She asked one question that shattered the idolatrous world I spent five plus years making, "Like Abraham, if God asked for this promise back, would you give it back to him? If not, you have made that thing an idol." In an instant just like I imagine it happened for the disciples in Luke 24:45, the eyes of my understanding were opened, and I realized I put this man before God. That night, I cried myself to sleep and the next day in a more sober mind, I got on my face and repented to God for the idol worship of marriage, the prophetic word and of this man. Immediately chains of desire for that man fell off me like two-ton weights–I felt lighter. I no longer desired to have him. While the desire for him died in that moment, I still had an obedience and ungodly desire for marriage. Recovering from my whole existence being about this man, a week later I decided to fast to get clarity on what exactly was happening. I felt the pressure of thousands of people that heard me openly declare on YouTube I knew who my husband was. As I fast and pray, the first thing I heard God say was to not question everything He's done these past few years in my life. The only area of deception I needed to concern myself with at the moment was the prophetic word of that man being my husband. I hear the Lord tell me He did suggest this man could be my husband, but it was only contingent upon his obedience and my obedience. The man didn't choose God and through my idol worship I didn't either. God said the prophetic word was revoked when I fell into unrepented sin–idolatry, and through the legal right of my sin (2 Thessalonians 2:9-12) the devil developed the lie. I was called to something, but like Moses, my own sin hindered me from stepping into it. God insisted He never told me I would be married in December 2021, nor half the other deceiving prophetic words I received after that. He consoled me in truth; He emphasized to me just how awful it was to see me disappointed time after time because of my own deception. As I spent time being built back up by God, repenting and renouncing the idol of that man, marriage, people and prophetic words, I began to get my strength back. The prophetic walls of God's voice became more fortified every day. In all humility, I made another YouTube video explaining the error of my ways. I also personally emailed and messaged all the women and men I lived in delusion with. I had to explain to them the deception I was in when I made my original video. Some wanted to step into the light of truth with me by submitting the person back to God to test the fruit, while some appreciated me reaching out, but would continue believing God for the spouse God showed them. Here is a good time to disclaim: I still believe that on occasion and to those who are faithful, God *does* reveal the identity of a future spouse. Here lately, I've been teaching the importance of vetting the prophetic word for an idolatry of marriage or any other idols in the hearts. While emphasizing how the information is not given to obsess over that person and/or make plans for the future, but rather to push harder in prayer. With a piece of information this important, prayer life must increase or that prophetic word and that person could easily become an idol.

After God sent me on a course correction and I turned from idolatry, I begged Him to let me delete the YouTube videos where I declare I knew who my husband was. He wouldn't let me, He said He would turn what was meant for evil for my good. In the days that shame wanted to overtake me as the video soared in numbers, God reminded me of His promise to redeem that time of deception. He kept that promise: In September 2022, one month after discovering my deception in August of 2022, a random man walking through his own journey of idolatry and deception would subscribe to my YouTube channel and follow me on social media based on those videos I begged God to delete. Two years after that, in August of 2024, that same man and I would connect and begin our journey towards forever. The very floor of marital shame that held my tears, would be my ceiling for marital blessing.

God Doesn't Force, He Proposes

There is an epidemic in the Chirstian community among singles, and it has got to be reckoned with. There's one side of the Kingdom that says, "God told me who my future spouse is" and there's another side that says, "God doesn't tell us who to marry." Then there's the truth. I believe the truth is somewhere in the middle; that's where I would like to live today. Are you willing?

Let me pour water on both parties' fire and say this: God makes suggestions concerning our future spouse, because we have free will and free choice (even to our own detriment). God doesn't force us to be with anyone. John 7:17 and Galatians 5:13 are examples of our free choice. If God doesn't force salvation onto us, why would we think He would force a marriage partner? The fairytales growing up led me to believe we only had one soul mate. In a perfect world, I believe this would be true; but because we live in a fallen world, there are people that don't choose partners out of healed places. Their souls are fragmented; thus, their mate's soul is too. Two fragmented souls wandering about for love. After many years of deception, what I know now is that God, in His sovereignty, has given us all purpose. On the journey of purpose there are people that He chooses to pair. Contingent upon both parties' obedience to God and agreement to pairing, they can be matched. Three times in my life I have heard the Lord suggest possible mates, at the time I didn't have the knowledge nor spiritual maturity to inquire what the process would look like. The first time, after months of continuing to hear of a possible match, I finally agreed. Only inquiring of the Lord for a few instructions, I didn't know the biggest and most important—don't make your desire for this person bigger than God, i.e. don't make them an idol. In my process of making them an idol, I also didn't realize this person was not choosing me, nor did I realize this was a mere suggestion from God, not an end all, be all. In between God's suggestions I dated a lot of frogs that clearly communicated to God and my friends I didn't know how to pick men correctly. I told God my picker was broken and that I wanted His help. The second time around I was hesitant, but I agreed with God quickly because I wanted what He wanted for me. Unlike the first time around, I began to date this man not knowing idolatry (people, marriage, lust) had crept back into my heart and was the gas fueling our relationship. As it all came to a turning point, in God's divine intervention of mercy, this choice did not choose me. I remember asking God why it was all happening, He said, "Kayla, I won't allow you to marry a disobedient man." God had given me free will to choose, but in my idolatry, I was blinded as to who this man was choosing to be—rebellious. Thank God that my prayers of intercession, the groans only the Holy Spirit could interpret, allowed God to step in and save me from my idol. Growing in knowledge with every adversity, as the third time rolled around and I found myself hyper-cognizant of idol worship, of choice, and discernment to see what was unspoken. My fear of God to lose this relationship and to hurt God by bowing down to another, I surrendered this relationship back to God as often as I remembered. I renounced my allegiance to marriage any time I felt it come up. Through knowledge, I was delivered (Proverbs 11:9) from idolatry and now I can call myself not only the bride of Christ, but someone's bone of their bone and flesh of their flesh. God wrote a prophetic word one year before I met my husband telling me the characteristics of my husband and how I could pray for him. This time unlike the last, I used the prophetic words as prayer points and surrendered them back to God as often as I remembered. In times past, when God has highlighted men to me as possible husbands I acted out of error and became obsessed with these men. I didn't know that God was merely suggesting and there was work that would have to be done on my part for his suggestion to come to pass. Thank God that in the cycle of idolatry of marriage, I was finally able to get off the train.

Here are two additional disclaimers I think are important:

1. There are kingdom couples that God intended to be with other spouses, but in their free will they chose another and God blessed their choice.

2. I fully believe there are a select few people that know who their future spouse is, but it comes with instructions that when not followed could be the gateway for sin. This process is also very nuanced for every specific person.

Before I agreed to converse with my husband, God emphasized that he was simply a choice. What set my husband apart from the rest was my knowledge of free choice as well as the way God spoke of him. I had never heard God speak so highly of a man. In my sober mind, I was able to read God's recommendation of this man, only to make a wise decision to move forward into the courtship phase. Even in my indecisiveness, God reiterated that I had an anointing of wife and that my husband had the anointing of husband. We could choose another spouse that would also come with another set of problems and proclivities as well, but we would live great lives. These talks from the Lord escorted me out of my fairytale land and sobered me up to God's desire for marriage. More than making me happy, it was about God doing a new thing in our bloodlines, about God's will being done on the Earth. I was able to choose my husband in a heart that had no idolatry of marriage in it. My husband and I chose one another and every day we intentionally choose one another.

Above we've just found the truth in the middle concerning God suggesting spouses, but I want to quickly point out the far-left extreme which houses deception. These are the people that believe they heard God tell them who their spouse is, but deception tells us it isn't God speaking to them. The sin of idolatry effectively moves throughout the hearts of believers because of deception. I alluded to this in chapter one and to even further reiterate; due to spiritual law, an open door to idolatry gives legal right for deception to come and further cement the idolatry. Deception is like numbing cream before a procedure. The procedure wouldn't be half as effective if the cream hadn't been a distraction. Idolatry was the sin I fell into; deception made that sin oblivious to me. You wonder how people who say they love God with their whole hearts can do the most vile things and not blink an eye–it's because they have been deceived. The spirit of deception is whispering to them and telling them they aren't in error. The spirit of deception is like wool over their eyes when they find scripture to support their sin. This spirit is so cunning it will have the righteous even second guessing the truth (Matthew 24:24). For those people who believe they heard God talking to them, it wasn't God, it was the demon attached to that idol. I caution all to test the spirit behind every person's, "God told me..."

"The coming of the lawless one is by the activity of Satan with all power and false signs and wonders, and with all wicked deception for those who are perishing, because they refused to love the truth and so be saved. Therefore God sends them a strong delusion, so that they may believe what is false, in order that all may be condemned who did not believe the truth but had pleasure in unrighteousness." 2 Thessalonians 2:9-12 (ESV)

"So will I choose their delusions, And bring their fears on them; Because, when I called, no one answered, When I spoke they did not hear; But they did evil before My eyes, And chose that in which I do not delight."" Isaiah 66:4 (NKJV)

""Son of man, these men have set up their idols in their hearts, and put before them that which causes them to stumble into iniqui-

ty. Should I let Myself be inquired of at all by them? "Therefore speak to them, and say to them, 'Thus says the Lord God: "Everyone of the house of Israel who sets up his idols in his heart, and puts before him what causes him to stumble into iniquity, and then comes to the prophet, I the Lord will answer him who comes, according to the multitude of his idols, that I may seize the house of Israel by their heart, because they are all estranged from Me by their idols."'" Ezekiel 14:3-5 (NKJV)

Two ways to know if this word concerning your future spouse's identity came from God:

-   Check the fruit. What fruit is being produced because of the word God spoke to you? Are you growing closer to him as you intercede for this future spouse, becoming a better person? Or are you stalking their social media and stuck in your imagination, dreaming of the day they'll be yours?

-   Surrender them. Can you surrender the word and person back to God? If God asked for this person back, even if they weren't yours yet, could you surrender them out of your heart?

The Unchosen Choice

I can talk about idolatry in this way because this is what I know. This was my way of life because of my own choices. I chose not to love the truth. The truth, "Thou shalt have no other gods before me" (Exodus 20:3 (KJV)). The inception of my idolatry happened in the hearts of generations far before I was born, but the perpetuation of it started with the idolatry of marriage. I'm grateful God never allowed me to marry my idols. What felt like rejection in one season, was unrealized protection in another season. I wanted to be with my idol more than I wanted to be with God. The residency in my heart that should have only been reserved for God was spoken for. I wanted God to give me the desire of my heart even if it killed me. What I thought was God's cruelty, what I felt was sadness and betrayal, was God's fatherly sovereignty. My reward for idolatry was to feel rejected and unchosen. While this doesn't seem like a great reward, the alternative was death, because of my sins. With every experience that almost ended up in marriage, I was rescued by God from these situations feeling rejected and unchosen. While I was grateful to be rescued and, yes, the pangs of heartbreak eventually wore off, the residue of rejection lingered. This was never God's intention, but always the enemy's. He didn't need to win the war, as long as he could inflict a battle wound that outlasted the spoils of war. Idolatry left me with a complex of inadequacy and rejection I should have never experienced. Men caused me to feel like I wasn't worthy to be chosen as their bride; the whole time God was in their shadow begging me to be *His*. I didn't know God wanted me to be His bride *first*, I didn't know I had a Bridegroom in Him. On my journey of feeling like an option by men, I was chosen by God.

Woman to Woman

"Only with your eyes shall you look, And see the reward of the wicked." Psalms 91:8 (NKJV)

Shirley Brown's song, *Woman to Woman* will forever live rent free in my head as someone who was in idolatry. I used to sway my hips as the beat dropped to this song, and while I still do occasionally, I can't help but think of the idolatry I used to be in. I pray you all are never on the Barbara or Shirley end of a woman to woman phone call like I've been in the past, because I don't wish this phone call on anyone. Barbara, like me, was probably oblivious to the idolatrous cesspool she stepped into. Let's look at the facts: Shirley paid this man's car note, bought all his clothes, provided every piece of food he ate. After all that, her man still cheated on her. Where is the limit? Where is the line? When do you choose yourself? Why was Shirley obedient to love from a man that couldn't stay faithful greater than her obedience to God, or at the very least the God-like royalty within herself? In fact, the note she found in her "man's" pocket was a warning from God, yet she turned responsibility to the other woman instead of the one who vowed to be faithful to her. God is a good father and, in His mercy, did He provide her ways of escape (1 Corinthians 10:13). If you're halfway through this section and you have no idea what song I'm referring to. Look up the lyrics to Woman to Woman by Shirley Bown. Now, back to my impromptu think piece on Shirley...

If you don't strive to have a relationship that resembles Christ and the church, go ahead and gracefully skip to the next chapter–this no longer concerns you. If you're interested in a Godly relationship, then your alarms should be going off at the fact that she did this for a man that never loved her–this is a clear indication of idolatry. She wanted to be loved so terribly, she wanted to be in a relationship so badly, she compromised herself. In God's eyes, as much as it pained Him to see His daughter hurt, she needed to feel the betrayal God felt. There's a quote by Tiffany Buckner I think is fitting for this think piece, "The reward for your idolatry is a narcissist." There is no proof in the song that Shirley's man was a narcissist. In an effort to not erroneously throw this word around, I won't call him that either. I will say, sometimes God will put us through a living hell in order for us to get to the darkness and search for the only everlasting light. I had the unfortunate experience of dating a narcissist and the recovery sometimes lasts longer than the relationship. The gaslighting, the control, the entitlement, the manipulation, the selfishness, the jealousy, the neediness, the emotional roller coaster. On multiple occasions, I found myself advocating for my needs only to end up apologizing for standing up for myself. In my desire to be married and to finally have a "man," I was being conditioned to end up like Shirley. I wasn't paying car notes, but being so blinded by my idolatry, that probably wasn't too far down the line. It wouldn't be until I asked God to deliver me from the relationship that He would reveal the man had been given over to a reprobate mind (Romans 1) because of his disobedience to God. Nothing I did or said could have made him choose me, when he hadn't yet chosen God. Wondering why this man would treat me like this, not knowing I was doing the exact same thing to God. Many days as God collected my tears in a bottle, I'm sure He thought, "How does it feel to be cheated on?" My experience with natural infidelity from this man was parallel to the spiritual adultery I afflicted on God. The cherry on top of my pile of spiritual adultery was the small glimpse of how God must have felt when I chose to make a covenant with a sorority. Kneeling at an altar during the initiation process while signing my name in a book, wearing white, and pledging my heart, my mind and my strength to a god that wasn't Him. In addition, I got an understanding of how God feels when He asks me to fast, but gluttony whispers to the god of my stomach and seduces me out of a fast (Philippians 3:19). Understanding that what I sow is what I reap but forgetting to apply that to my relationship with God. Sowing mal-treatment to God and reaping mal-treatment from man was my reward. In my weeks of tearful repentance to God, He graced me to hear a message, and I was able to hear the revelation that would change my life. Beyond infidelity being the reward for my idolatry, why is it that in every relationship or "situationship" I've been in, I was cheated on? Through the prophet of God, He revealed there was a residue in the spirit that carried the scent of adultery and I was its target. Because of it, adulterous men were only ever attracted to me. In fact, I am convinced by the spirit that this residue blinded my husband who followed me on social media for two years from knowing me as *his wife,* this residue had me hidden. It wouldn't be until I asked God to cleanse me and make me clean from all residue of idolatry, adultery, and whatever other generational patterns that led to the destruction of marriages was I found to be a good thing by my husband.

So, woman to woman and even woman to man, if you are currently in a situation like Shirley's I want to kindly encourage you to choose yourself, more importantly, choose God and leave. It's time to move around from toxic relationships and leeching people that will never love you, only wound you.

This might be a good time to reflect on the dating patterns you have experienced and perpetuated thus far...

If They Knew Better, They Would Do Better

"The greater my wisdom, the greater my grief. To increase knowledge only increases sorrow." Ecclesiastes 1:18 (NLT)

The only thing equally worse than living in idolatry is watching those whom you love live blissfully in the ignorance of idolatry. There is a unique affliction of having to see someone you love receive their reward for idolatry and not being able to intervene. Having to watch them walk through their pain from a horizontal and sometimes aerial point of view in prayer because it's not *your* idolatry, thus it's not *your* war to win. The agony of not being able to get into the fight with them because you have been sanctified; no longer forcing God to make war with your idols that get in His way. This is a unique pain that I don't wish on anyone. In contrast, there are times when God asks you to fight for someone through intercession because He's called you to be a wailing watchman on the wall. Time spent in prayer, begging God to relent. Asking God for mercy, not realizing mercy is that He didn't kill them immediately for their adultery towards Him. In His mercy, their slap on the wrist for idolatry is that they *get* to experience a reward of suffering with an expected end date. Suffering that won't kill them. Their flesh maybe, but their lamp stand won't be removed.

This unique stance sent me into a prayer of questions:

God, how do I endure watching the people I love suffer for their idolatry? How do I watch them endure this pain? How do I know when to walk beside them in prayer or like Jeremiah not to pray for them any longer (Jeremiah 7:16 & 11:14)? God, would you have mercy on them? God, why is this happening to them; they're a good person? God, please relent. God, if you choose not to have mercy on them, would you help me to be okay with their consequences?

This is when God answered me like He did Job in Job chapters 38-41. God was heavy on the, "Who is this that speaks with words without knowledge." Thinking He would answer my questions, He flips it and asks, *"How is it that you can cry for your loved ones that are experiencing sadness because of their sins and idolatry, yet have no tears for me? How do you think it makes me feel to punish them because of the spiritual law you all live by? More importantly, how do you think it feels to be cheated on by the very bride my son died for? You have no pity on my heart? All your pity goes to my people. Why is that? Why is it that you think you are the only one that grieves when they go against my precepts? I hurt too. I'm not such a terrible God that I don't emote. It's clear you think you're their "god", and now through your prayer it's confirmed you have become a Demigod. You think if you don't carry them through this, they'll fall and die? You think you're their savior? What cross did you die on? Where are your stripes that healed my people? I know the world calls you an empath, but too often empaths walk in pride; they think they're the healers. With this mindset a Lucifer fall is imminent. Never think of yourself as irreplaceable. If you don't pray for them, their father, Abba, Me, I will catch them when they fall. Yes, you are to be an intercessor but understand your spiritual role in the courtroom of Heaven. You are simply a lobbyist, an advocate at best. You bring their problem to the judge and plead on their be-*

half in prayer. You aren't the judge and you aren't their god. I, the judge, slam the gavel down and render them guilty or innocent. While Satan, the accuser of the brethren and you present the evidence. Stay in your lane, Kayla."

For those of you that felt a heavy conviction in your chest, this might be a good place to repent for every time you thought if you didn't pray, if you didn't save, if you didn't help, your Father's other child, wouldn't be prayed for by their personal intercessor–Holy Spirit. They were saved by grace through the faith of Jesus Christ; shame on you and me for thinking you are the ancient of days, the great I am.

Now that we've repented. Don't rest in that shame or the burden of others. Incorporate the information you've learned into the next time you have a desire to play hero.

Indication You Have an Idolatry of Marriage

As God silenced a nation because of their idolatry, He took celebrations, joy and marriages from them. No longer was there heard the voice of the bride and the bridegroom. This directly translates to modern day. Have you ever seen a family where no one is married? A family where everyone is single? This is proof there is a curse of idolatry within the family. Just as we read in Jeremiah about God silencing the voice of the bride and bridegroom, it is happening currently.

Below are ten indications you could be living in an idolatry of marriage.

1. Marriage is all you ever think about.

2. Constant extreme sadness, frustration, and/or discontentment as a result of singleness.

3. A disproportionate number of your goals are related to your relationship status.

4. Willing to settle for almost right.

5. Ignoring red flags, thinking the person will change or you can, "pray" them through.

6. A tendency to modify your personality, likes, dislikes, styles, etc. to align with a potential date.

7. Choosing a significant other based on your ability to marry faster rather than being led by God.

8. A distrust or inconsistency of God because of singleness.

9. Willingness to disobey God to please your spouse or significant other.

10. You are not living in freedom of 1 Corinthians 7:32-34.

"I want you to be free from the concerns of this life. An unmarried man can spend his time doing the Lord's work and thinking how to please him. But a married man has to think about his earthly responsibilities and how to please his wife. His interests are divided. In the same way, a woman who is no longer married or has never been married can be devoted to the Lord and holy in body and in spirit. But a married woman has to think about her earthly responsibilities and how to please her husband." 1 Corinthians 7:32-34 (NLT)

This scripture outlines the task of an unmarried man and woman–pleasing the Lord. There is an order to the Kingdom, and this is a necessary step. If someone cannot be faithful to God in covenant, they can never be faithful to their spouse in marriage.

Story time: A very comical/unserious indication I was in idolatry:

Whilst I was in the depths of idolatry, the belly of Sheol some might say, the one factor that alerted me that something wasn't right was when the idolatry went against my natural way of life. I'm a cheapskate at heart. I like to ball out, but, when necessary, I will pinch a penny with no regrets. When grocery shopping, sometimes I would purchase discounted meat that needs to be cooked or frozen on that day. I picked up the habit in college and carried it into early postgrad. In the midst of my sorry attempt at trying to be a "wife", but no wifey benefits, I was delusionally cooking a man dinner. As I had the meat defrosting, he saw the expiration tag and threw my meat away. He proceeded to "clean out" my freezer and threw three additional packs of meat away with no intent to replace them—I said nothing. I realize some of you might agree with him and maybe he was saving our lives, but my mom is from the country in North Carolina, and she taught me her country ways; this was absurd to me. One of these days I will forgive myself for being so blinded by the possibility of love.

What are some moments from your past relationships that confirm you were in idolatry?

What Idolatry Eventually Made Me Do

Jeremiah writes that when God's people repented for their idolatry, that's when the curse of idolatry was lifted. In the land where there were no marriages, they were able to marry again because God could trust their hearts with the gift and assignment of marriage.

""Thus says the Lord: 'Again there shall be heard in this place —of which you say, "It is desolate, without man and without beast"—in the cities of Judah, in the streets of Jerusalem that are desolate, without man and without inhabitant and without beast, the voice of joy and the voice of gladness, the voice of the bridegroom and the voice of the bride, the voice of those who will say: "Praise the Lord of hosts, For the Lord is good, For His mercy endures forever"— and of those who will bring the sacrifice of praise into the house of the Lord. For I will cause the captives of the land to return as at the first,' says the Lord." Jeremiah 33:10-11 (NKJV)

After experiencing the consequences for my idolatry of marriage, I vowed to never go back. As I processed through the early stages of dating and courting my husband, my idolatrous past forced me closer to God. I had such a fear of displeasing God, I wouldn't allow myself to put a man back on the throne of my heart. I couldn't risk betraying my Father in Heaven. Past idolatry forced me to keep God first. I put boundaries in place so I wouldn't end up falling back into idolatry. I spent more time with God because I saw that through Him, I was able to love my spouse more. My idolatrous past made me cognizant of my priorities. It also taught me the difference between balance and priority. I balance my job, family, relationships, etc., but I prioritize God, after God I prioritize my husband. Lastly, it taught me just how much I hurt God's feelings by choosing things and people over Him. Now, as a married woman, because I've asked God to keep me from idolizing a man, specifically, my man; my relationship with my husband is only as good as my relationship with God. Oftentimes when I do something to deeply hurt or offend my husband, the first person I know I must apologize to is God. Chances are, I've hurt Him first. He communicates with me through my relationship with my husband. For example, there was a time my husband asked me not to do something and I did it anyway. When the consequences of my disobedience caught up to me, I cried in God's face wondering why I'd been forsaken (I'm also very dramatic). Holy Spirit spoke so clearly to me saying, "You treat me the same way. You disrespect me the same way." I could no longer live in victim mode. I had to humble myself and apologize to my Heavenly husband and my Earthly husband.

I thank God for my idolatry meter in the form of my Earthly husband, Deion. God uses my marriage to sanctify me. While it does not always feel good, it is necessary.

Idolatry of Lust

Lust is defined as: very strong sexual desire.

Perversion is defined as: the alteration of something from its original course, meaning, or state to a distortion or corruption of what was first intended.

Lust Defined

Lust is a common spirit that, like most fungi, lives in dark places, but can be easily spotted. Unlike certain traits of Leviathan and Jezebel, lust can be extremely and completely obvious. On the opposite end of the spectrum there are times when it is occultic and completely undetected. In those cases, most may be completely oblivious to it, while the patriarchs, matriarchs, and other members of the family act as if their bloodline isn't infested with it. Infested with workers of iniquity that show up for an evil day's work when the sun comes up only to rock you to sleep at night. In addition, they expect their time and a half pay on holidays when the whole bloodline gathers, quietly observing their work in concert. I know this spirit all too well, I, like many of you, were born into it.

How Lust Manifested in My Life

My parents were also born into it, more than likely their parents as well–a cyclical gift one might say. Trying to pinpoint where it entered in on a bloodline, while important, might prove to be futile, especially if your family is vault-like. What's essential is where it ends. If you're reading this, my hope is that it ends with you.

Lust Is Not a Character Flaw, It Is a Heart Issue

Lust entered my life well before I was thought of by my parents, when the Bible says that God knew us before we were formed in our mother's womb (Jeremiah 1:5), the enemy also knew us. He's not omnipresent or all-knowing like our God, but he knew someone, a deliverer, a repairer of broken walls was being formed, he just didn't know who or when. Similar to Pharaoh when Moses was being born and King Herod when Jesus was being born. The avenue in which the enemy has consistently tried to take my life was through the spirit of lust. He was unsuccessful at killing my parents, unsuccessful at my birth, and has been unsuccessful at killing me since then. Lust manifested in my life at a young age. I was exposed to pornography very early on and the exposure awoke a desire in me that would grow with me into my adolescent years until one day, the Lord took the desire from my heart and I didn't look back. Self-pleasure would keep me in bondage for years. I'll spare the additional details, but I knew things I shouldn't have known and saw things I shouldn't have seen. As a child, I was ignorant to the magnitude of just how evil my desires were, but I didn't know I was named in a perverse contract written in blood on my bloodline. I thought it was *just* me; I thought my heart had conceived this sin and according to the Bible I deserved death. I didn't know this was a contract that named my whole bloodline in the covenant. As a young person, in my condemnation I thought, *how could I ever get married and have a normal life living this lie*. Not knowing it was on the bloodline, I didn't know I was simply living out what I was born into. The difference was that *my* conviction set in early as a child because I was born to be set apart, to be called out from among them. Back in 2023 in my God says journal, I asked God, "Who is Kayla Fontino"? The Lord said, "I've had to contend with the enemy over her. He wanted her so badly, but my warring angel was always on guard. Even when it looked like the enemy won, he didn't…" When Holy Spirit wrote this and even now, I can't help but think about the ways in which the enemy wanted me and planned to take me out through lust, through perversion, rape, molestation, incest, etc. A slow death it would have been, he would have taken my mind first, my way of life would have reflected satan, then my body, finally, my soul. But God, in His mercy, even when it looked like satan won, my redeemer held the victorious battle axe. When I became of age in the church, Psalms 51 was my repentance scripture after every lustful indiscretion. I often felt like King David, a slave to lust. Even though I married as a virgin, the Lord was clear when He said, "But I say unto you, that whosoever looketh on a woman to lust after her hath committed adultery with her already in his heart" Matthew 5:28 *(KJV)*. The world saw me as pure, but sometimes in my heart, I was no purer than a prostitute. How I managed to maintain my "purity" was at no hand of my own. In moments of passion with men who promised me the world, Holy Spirit's convictions were always louder than their whispers. In 2022, a few years after I started my YouTube channel, the Lord spoke to me with a warning, "If you have sex out of wedlock, you will immediately become pregnant." This message from God came because while I was on my channel encouraging the women and men of God to abstain from sex, create sexual boundaries, etc. I was considering the opposite. Holy Spirit wouldn't let me be a hypocrite. Immediately, I knew this to be a warning, not a threat; threats can be general and sometimes empty, warnings are concise–God wasn't playing with me. I knew in my disobedience to have sex before I married would end in me hosting a *Waiting Well* book signing followed by a baby shower designed for an unwed mother; the forethought of shame and disappointment was enough to keep my legs closed. Again, this didn't make me pure. Purity was a heart posture that I simply didn't possess. I knew I had to contend with this heart posture before I married and before I had children. I knew whatever giant I didn't slay, would double in size at the joining in holy matrimony with my husband. Additionally, I knew those same giants would make my children public enemy number one. Honestly, it's not that I didn't want to marry or even have the opportunities to marry, I simply knew I couldn't marry without this victory over lust under my belt. Before I married, I went on a fast to kill and defeat lust and perversion. Throughout the fast I learned that I would need maintenance from lust and perversion because that spirit is a sneaky one. When the fast was over, I felt from the Lord that with His help, I slayed the giant of lust, and my children would not have to contend with it *like* I did. I'm grateful to God it ends with me. God did His part, now my lifestyle must reflect one who keeps boundaries in place, especially the things I allow through my ear and eye gates.

The Idol of Lust: Is Lust Your God?

"Therefore let him who thinks he stands take heed lest he fall. No temptation has overtaken you except such as is common to man; but God is faithful, who will not allow you to be tempted beyond what you are able, but with the temptation will also make the way of escape, that you may be able to bear it. Therefore, my beloved, flee from idolatry." I Corinthians 10:12-14 (NKJV)

As time has gone by and my revelation of how I let lust rule my life has become evident. As a child I was ignorant, but as an adult, I chose to sin. I put the god of lust before God, and I worshiped *it* instead of God. Maybe I didn't bow down to it in a literal sense, but figuratively, I actively chose to participate in that which I knew would make my God jealous. In Exodus 20:3 *(NKJV)* God says, "You shall have no other gods before Me." When I pleasured myself or allowed someone to do it outside of marriage, I put my lust before the Lord. Not realizing as Jesus' bride in the new covenant, sex outside of the covenant of marriage made me an adulterer. I was living a life of infidelity, not even comprehending that my thoughts of fornication *were* idolatry. Not understanding that the way lust preoccupied my mind was my worship to it. Nor did I realize how jealous it made God to see me given over to the lust of my flesh. I confused the one and true living God with the god of this world. The god of this world didn't mind a polyamorous relationship, offering my body to God as a living sacrifice on Sunday, then offering my body to a man or myself Monday-Saturday. The god of this world kept me in a haze of deception, allowing me just enough holy to praise God AND my fleshly desires. Not realizing the character of *my* God says I cannot worship both. Satan didn't mind that I was a regular church goer, as long as he held my heart captive from God through lust. Satan knew the Bible more than I did. He knew if he could keep me preoccupied with the works of serving God, yet have my heart far from God with sin, that would be enough for me to be rejected by God on the day of judgement (Matthew 7:21-23). With God's help, I was able to stand from my bowed position to the god of lust. As God showed me the land I was delayed in possessing because of my sin, I realized my decision to stand up from the god of lust allowed me to be seated next to Christ. It's not easy, but like any maintenance from deliverance, it's not supposed to be easy, it's supposed to take faith. There is a clear divide like never before in the body of Christ, those who have bowed down to the god of lust and those who are seated next to Christ, whose side will you be on? I'm on the Lord's side–I bow for God and only God.

Lust x Rejection

What spirit taunts you with worthlessness, dangles your lack of acceptance in your face, preys on your biggest fears, makes you feel as if you're an outcast, all while encouraging you to question your identity. What is the spirit of rejection for 300?

Rejection is all throughout the Bible, Ishmel was rejected by Abraham. Leah was rejected by Jacob. The Children of Israel often rejected God. Rejection is, unfortunately all around us, never failing to make us feel like the gum on the bottom of someone's shoe or a penny with a hole in it.

David is my favorite Bible character. Early on in my "serious" Christian walk I found so much of myself in David. He was a man after God's own heart (1 Samuel 13:14). I've always felt like I was a *woman* after God's own heart. In my reading and synthesizing the Bible, I figured David was a man after God's own heart because of how he worshiped God, nobody danced like David. Nobody repented and drew closer to God in their sorrow like David. As my studying increased and as Holy Spirit shared more, I've come to realize an additional reason why God considered David a man after His own heart. God, like David, understood what it was to be rejected. *"And the Lord said to Samuel, "Heed the voice of the people in all that they say to you; for they have not rejected you, but they have rejected Me, that I should not reign over them." 1 Samuel 8:7 (NKJV).* All throughout David's life he was rejected, while the Bible doesn't explicitly say, "David was rejected." We see the first sighting of this when all of David's brothers are brought in to stand before Samuel as king prospects. David's own father disregarded his presence and failed to ask him to be considered (1 Samuel 16). This behavior from his father Jesse would explain many theologians' point when they argue whether David's mother and father were married when they conceived him (See Psalms 51:5). Likewise, there is also scripture to prove his parents were legitimately married (See Psalms 69:8 & 1 Samuel 22:3-4). I'm not 100% certain of the relationship status of his parents, what I am certain of is the spirit of rejection that stalked him. There is additional proof of his familial positioning within the interactions of him and his brothers when he goes to take his brothers food in their battle against Goliath and the Philistines (1 Samuel 17:28-29). We see another sighting of rejection in 1 Samuel 18 when David was promised Saul's older daughter, Merab, but she's given to someone else. In 1 Samuel 19, David was told that Saul wanted him dead and Saul made an attempt on his life, but David fled. In 1 Samuel 20:1, we hear of David's frustration and confusion as to why Saul seeks his life. Again, this frustration and confusion is voiced in 1 Samuel 24, but this time to Saul himself as David had just spared his life from death. This happens again in 1 Samuel 26. As a therapist, but also as a Bible scholar, I'm interested in what encouraged David to continuously pursue Saul's acceptance after he was rejected so many times. My guess is that Saul initially gave David what his father Jesse never did–honor. Saul did everything, but crown David as king. This positive, fatherly attention more than likely soothed a place in David's soul his own father failed to do. What David thought was the supplement to his fatherly wound of rejection only cut him deeper. David loved being all that King Saul needed, especially his son-in-law (1 Samuel 18:23), but in Saul's jealousy did he ruin this for David. As if rejection from his own family wasn't enough, in keeping with the spirit of rejection present in David's life, he found refuge with the Philistines who eventually rejected him as well (1 Samuel 27 & 29). *"Then Achish called David and said to him, "Surely, as the Lord lives, you have been upright, and your going out and your coming in with me in the army is good in my sight. For to this day I have not found evil in you since the day of your coming to me. Nevertheless the lords do not favor you. Therefore return now, and go in peace, that you may not displease the lords of the Philistines." So David said to Achish, "But what have I done? And to this day what have you found in your servant as long as I have been with you, that I may not go and fight against the enemies of my lord the king?" Then Achish answered and said to David, "I know that you are as good in my sight as an angel of God; nevertheless the princes of the Philistines have said, 'He shall not go up with us to the battle.'"1 Samuel 29:6-9 (NKJV).* David's plea with Achish is painful to read because the rejection is amplified. If it was just Saul or his family that rejected him, we could argue the absence of the spirit of rejection in David's life, but these encounters with the Philistines make it clear there is a *spirit* of David contended with. The patterns in his life are undeniable; first his father, then Saul, then the Philistines, with other small but impactful instances of rejection in between. David's poetry in the book of Psalms also proves David's rejection as it is full of pain, sorrow, and rejection; Psalms 118:22 is an example of this. God recognized himself in David's heart when he still chose to serve even when the person he was serving hated him. God recognized David's integrity not to kill Saul, simply because he was one God had chosen. David is a man after God's own heart because when God looked at David's heart, He saw His own and our Father can't say that about just anyone's heart.

While side effects of rejection come in many shapes and sizes, For David, it showed up as lust. The fruit of emptiness from his tree of rejection left an unattainable attempt to be filled. David, like so many, looked for that fulfillment in sex. He seemed to only feel true acceptance in bed. Even as the worshipper David was, his love for God couldn't quench the thirst of the traumatic neglect his family left. Not even the covenant could deter the lust of his flesh. He saw Bathsheba and took her for himself even though she was already spoken for. Being married himself wasn't even able to eradicate the lust that was on parade.

Find Your Own Strongman

Rejection was the strongman and lust was one of the many lieutenants operating within David. As we read of David, lust masquerades as the head honcho, but with a closer look into David's life it is clear it is a smoke screen for the true control center operator. What is the root cause of lust for you? Rejection, unforgiveness, pride, perversion, fear, trauma-abuse, emotional instability, selfishness, lack of self-control, etc. It is important not to be fooled by the enemy and his cunning schemes to distract with symptoms from the actual nucleus of the problem. Be vigilant and walk closely with Holy Spirit in wisdom as you interview yourself, so as not to fall victim to an answer from the third or fourth spirit in command. E.g. don't let the sacrificial spirit of lying or murder wear you out by convincing you he's the boss when really his paycheck is written like everyone else's. In your due diligence, command to speak to the strongman and when you do, have your axe in hand to uproot him in the authority of Jesus Christ where he stands.

____

____

____

____

____

____

____

____

____

____

____

The Compromise of Lust

'Then it happened one evening that David arose from his bed and walked on the roof of the king's house. And from the roof he saw a woman bathing, and the woman was very beautiful to behold. So David sent and inquired about the woman. And someone said, " Is this not Bathsheba, the daughter of Eliam, the wife of Uriah the Hittite?" Then David sent messengers, and took her; and she came to him, and he lay with her, for she was cleansed from her impurity; and she returned to her house. And the woman conceived; so she sent and told David, and said, "I am with child."' II Samuel 11:2-5 (NKJV)

Throughout this situation, we see that lust compromised David in a way that was irreversible. Not only did the spirit of lust come with a spirit of murder, but also a spirit of lying. This lust brought shame to his name and scandal to his household. In Revelation 2:12-17, God writes a letter to the compromised church. He explains to them how they held the doctrine of Balaam–the prophet in Numbers 22-24 who saw the line of sin and wondered how close he could get before it was considered sin. Balaam was willing to do anything for a dollar, to feed that lust of money, the root of all evil. With every concession, David fell deeper into compromise. In a season when David should have been away at war, he thought it better to stay home, a concession. David saw a woman that was already married and slept with her anyway, a compromise. David found out she was pregnant and sought to cover it up, a concession. Uriah, Bathsheba's husband, was a righteous man so David had him killed, a compromise. Lust always demands a compromise. It calls for a lower caliber of integrity. Lust never travels alone, always with a battle buddy ready to nail the coffin shut on their victim's destiny.

As I stated earlier, David is the Bible character I can relate to the most because he too struggled with lust. By the time he asked

God to take it from him, it was too late. Lust not only caused the kingdom to be ripped from his hands, but ultimately, he passed it down to his offspring. As I studied first and second Samuel, Kings, and Chronicles, I was amazed at how someone so favored could still be so flawed. This gave me solace that while God is just and sovereign, He's also merciful. Understanding our human proclivities and still loving us anyway. Reading what became of David's life and lineage because of lust had the same effect on me as the show *Scared Straight*. Because of David's example, I've sought to find the nearest exit off the pathway of destruction. I see how the enemy has had me in his grasp and I don't want that for my children. I've worked diligently to be delivered and to maintain my deliverance from lust, although I have been able to do nothing without God giving me the power and the desire to do so. Everything I do, every fast I complete, every prayer I pray, is so my children won't be sifted like wheat for the consequences of lust *I* failed to confront. David gave the devil hell in every other way except when it came to the spirit of lust. David closed all doors, but the devil found a window in which he would use to implode David's life. I once heard a prophet say, "Whatever you don't kill will seek to kill your children..." King Saul didn't kill all the Amalekites. Who he didn't obediently kill in 1 Samuel 15, showed up in 1 Samuel 30 to take David and his soldier's wives and children. What is it that you need to kill before it kills your children?

The Consequences of Lust

"When lust is uncontained, you cannot control what it produces."
-Unknown

The consequences of lust include but is not limited to: sex outside of marriage, STDs/STI, children out of wedlock, abortion, delay, adultery, infidelity, perversion, rape, incest, molestation, idolatry, bitterness, sickness, mental illness, death, and so much more.

Lust is the gateway drug no D.A.R.E officers think to mention. Romans 6:23 tells us that the wages of sin is death. When lust is present, we don't get to dictate what type of death we experience. This could be a physical death, ask Ananias and Sapphira in Acts 5. A spiritual death, ask Saul in 1 Samuel 16. A mental death, ask king Nebuchadnezzar. A death to the bloodline, ask Eli in 1 Samuel 3 and Pharaoh in Exodus 11. A financial death, ask Judas in Matthew 27. A painful death, ask Haman in Esther 7. An emotional death, ask Lot's wife in Genesis 19. The greatest deception is with those who think they can get away with their sins, but Psalms 37:7 tells us not to fret because of those who seem to get away with evil. God's grace and on occasion, generational habits of our bloodline determine the punishment. This is why some people can commit a sin and drop dead, while others seemingly play in God's face without punishment. Be not deceived, their day of judgement is coming, but in God's allegiance and covenant with their praying grandparents and/or parents God is giving them time to repent (2 Peter 3:9). Those with a history of witchcraft and occult practices might commit a sin and give up the ghost. It truly just depends on what is in the bloodline. David thought his t's were crossed and his i's were dotted, but El Roi–the God who sees, saw everything. He searched David's heart and knew his wicked ways even before conception. We also cannot dictate how far the sin of lust travels through perversion; I can imagine David never thought the wages of his sin would lead to the incest and rape of his daughter and eventually to the murder of not one son, but three.

Below is a scriptural back story and timeline of how lust and the consequences of lust were present throughout David's offspring's life:

David had two wives by 1 Samuel 25:39–Ahinoam of Jezreel and Abigail, Nabal's widow. He would have had three because he was married to Michal, Saul's daughter, but after attempting to kill

David, Saul gave his daughter Michal to another man. In 2 Samuel 3:13-16, David took Michal from her husband, and she became his wife again. By 2 Samuel 3, Maakah, Haggith, Abital, and Eglah became David's wives while he was in exile. By 2 Samuel 11, Bathsheba became the final wife to be highlighted in the Bible to David, although Abishag was noted to lay with him in his last days (1 King 1). While unnamed there are more than likely several concubines David had that produced children. As you read the scriptural timeline, it's important to note that David's children were written into a perverse contract the minute he committed adultery. Death was established over his house the minute he ordered Uriah, a faithful husband and servant in the Lord's army, to be killed. David's children were only doing what was written in blood for their bloodline. David slayed giants, but the biggest giant he failed to slay was the giant of his flesh.

Timeline:

- David has sex with Bathsheba and she conceives a son.

- David gets Bathsheba's husband killed.

- The son David has with Bathsheba dies.

- David is warned by Prophet Nathan that evil is coming out of his house because of his sins.

- In God's mercy does He allow Bathsheba to conceive again, giving birth to Solomon, whom God loved.

- David's son Ammon rapes David's daughter, Tamar.

- While angry, David did not punish Ammon.

- Absalom, David's son and brother to Tamar, kills their brother Ammon two years later.

- Solomon's love for foreign women turns his heart from God.

- The kingdom is torn away and given to Solomon's servants –all except for one tribe (Judah) because of God's covenant to David.

- Rehoboam, Solomon's son, took eighteen wives and sixty concubines. He had twenty-eight sons and sixty daughters (2 Chronicles 11:21).

- Solomon's grandchildren were given many wives by their father, Rehoboam (2 Chronicles 11:23).

Below I outlined some additional consequences of lust:

- Quenching Holy Spirit

- Abortions: "In addition to sexual rituals, Moloch worship included child sacrifice, or "passing children through the fire." It is believed that idols of Moloch were giant metal statues of a man with a bull's head. Each image had a hole in the abdomen and possibly outstretched forearms that made a kind of ramp to the hole. A fire was lit in or around the statue. Babies were placed in the statue's arms or in the hole. When a couple sacrificed their firstborn, they believed that Moloch would ensure financial prosperity for the family and future children (GotQuestions.org, 2022).[1]

- Children out of wedlock

- Broken structure of Christ and the church

- Adultery

- Idolatry in multiple areas

- Wages of sin=death

---

[1] GotQuestions.org. (2022, January 4). GotQuestions.org. https://www.gotquestions.org/child-sacrifice.html

PSA

'*"Don't pick on people, jump on their failures, criticize their faults —unless, of course, you want the same treatment. Don't condemn those who are down; that hardness can boomerang. Be easy on people; you'll find life a lot easier. Give away your life; you'll find life given back, but not merely given back—given back with bonus and blessing. Giving, not getting, is the way. Generosity begets generosity."* Luke 6:37 (MSG)

A public service announcement to all my parents that are saved, sanctified, filled with the Holy Ghost, et cetera, et cetera. Please stop demonizing your children for sins that you: One, initiated into the bloodline, or two, failed to contend with on the bloodline. When the same lust that is in you (active or dormant) shows up in your child how dare you judge and punish your child for something they possess quite honestly. Your children were named in a perverse and evil contract that you have yet to break and renounce. Stop making your child feel like a heathen for the feelings or thoughts they're experiencing. In addition, what will prove ineffective and unsuccessful is you pushing your fears onto them, locking them in the house, making them wear overly modest clothes, or threatening them into submission, dehumanizing the opposite sex will not stop the curiosity either. It's important to note, parents usually bomb in this area because they push their fears onto their children; your deepest fear is your child becoming you. In your race to see your fears not actualize, you are creating another you in the process. Fighting the process in all the wrong ways. Don't contend with your child, contend with that spirit. Give them the gift you needed but never got as a child–deliverance. Walk them through the process of deliverance (please don't do this if you have not been delivered yourself) and I caution you to make this as non-traumatic as possible. Simply having them repeat a repentance and renunciation prayer after you is a great start. Furthermore, seek God on whether your child needs deliverance from lust or simply has a healthy curiosity. If you don't begin the conversation around sex, they will find the answers in the world. The world will show them sex in a perverse, demonic way. When really, sex is something God created for a bride and bridegroom to enjoy in the confines of the marriage bed. Share with them how sex can be a wonderful worship experience between man and wife and should be reserved only for man and wife. Plant seeds in them about how it's God's intention for them to marry and have sex with one woman or man for the rest of their life and as God's will be done in their life they will enjoy their God-given spouse. Also share with them how when sin entered the world, God's intentions were perverted and this is where lusts of the flesh came in. Share with them how while it is not God's design, some people do have sex outside of marriage but also instill in them how this is not an option for them, nor one the Lord would like them to take. Be honest with them about how this was an option you took or wanted to, but didn't, or by the grace of God simply didn't take. You are their first teacher, and they will do as you do, not as you say. This might even mean you will need to openly repent for bringing men/women in and out of your home and explain your newfound abstinence journey if applicable. Lastly, share your experiences, regrets and opinions honest Biblical truths about sex. To clarify, your opinions are no good on a subject God has already spoken on, especially they are contrary to what the Lord has declared. Start a generational blessing of transparency and healthy conversations amongst parents and children in your bloodline. The real flex in parenthood is when the world exposes your child to sex and/or lust of the flesh, and your child comes to you with their questions or is already informed on what it is they were exposed to. While everyone else is being taught by the internet, causing more loss of innocence, your child has a teacher in their parent. This conversation starts as early as they can talk and walk. No, this doesn't involve you telling a 4-year-old the intricacies of a sexual experience between a man and a woman, but it will include you naming the sexual organs God gave them, boundaries, consent, etc... As they grow, this conversation matures. Wait until they are a teenager to have this conversation and you'll find your teen telling you all there is to know about sex instead of the other way around. It's worth noting, this conversation is different with every child. We all learn and process information differently. Be led by the Holy Spirit on how to approach these conversations with your specific child–don't traumatize them in efforts to educate them.

I'm already proud of you because you're already leaps and bounds ahead of the previous generation. What happened to you won't happen to your children, in the name of Jesus. I'm excited for your bloodline–it needed a repairer of the breech like you! You've taken the steps to be delivered from your own trauma and the covenants and symptoms your trauma brought. Now you are a better child of God, friend, sibling, spouse, parent, leader, employee and employer because of it. May God bless you in your efforts as you evolve into the best version of yourself.

A PSA to the PSA

Cover your child's gates. What have they heard, seen, spoken and come into agreement with that is coming to kill, steal and destroy them? God has given and entrusted you with spiritual authority over their life. Some things won't come out, but through prayer and fasting. Yes, your child can fast, if they can tell you "no" and throw a tantrum, they can fast. In the book of Jonah 4 and in 2 Chronicles 20, the kings made everyone, from the greatest to the least, go on a fast because their lives were in the balance. How much is your bloodline's freedom worth? No excuses, kill your flesh and have your child kill their flesh as well–give them the generational gift of fasting. While you, the parent are more than likely doing the Biblical definition of a fast (abstain from all foods and sometimes water for a period of time) but your child can start off at an appropriate level: this could look like having them fast for an hour or three, having them fast from sweets or processed foods, having them fast from their favorite food or snack, etc. Seek the great physician (Luke 5:31) if you or your child has a medical ailment, but again, make no excuses. Your child might fight you on this, but it's not their spirit, it's their flesh (1 Corinthians 9:27).

God doesn't despise the small beginnings, so neither should you–start off small concerning their fast as your child grows in the faith. As they fast, teach them Godly habits for praying and fasting. Teach them to memorize two or three scriptures they can recite during the fast for the thing they're believing in. Write down or have them write down what they are believing for; when it comes to pass, as you worship God, explicitly show them what their faith in God produced. They will rise up and call you blessed because of your stewardship over them.

Lastly, as I mentioned earlier: mom/dad, you're doing a great job, and I am so proud of you, more importantly your Father in Heaven is proud of you. God has given you this child. No matter the many mistakes you have made, with every new day, there is mercy and you have an opportunity to become a better you.

Restoration

"So I will restore to you the years that the swarming locust has eaten, The crawling locust, The consuming locust, And the chewing locust, My great army which I sent among you. You shall eat in plenty and be satisfied, And praise the name of the Lord your God, Who has dealt wondrously with you; And My people shall never be put to shame." Joel 2:25-26 (NKJV)

For those that experience lust like David did, his story didn't end in destruction. God's restoration for David was painful, embarrassing and public. He lost three children and his daughter lived with her defilement. Yet the most important thing is that God spared David's life and gave him an opportunity to turn from sin. "...God didn't only want to heal David of the *guilt* of his sin; He also wanted to heal David of the *presence* of this sin. We never read of David committing adultery again because God used these chastisements to drive such impurities far from David" (David Guzik, 2025).[2]

David's restoration process was so painfully beautiful because what separated David and other people of God who died in their sin was David's heart posture and conviction. We see that Saul lost his conviction and because of this God gave him over to a tormenting spirit, a reprobate mind. We should all strive to have a heart of deep repentance like David had. We should also seek to follow David's restorative process. With restoration came repentance and a deliverance process. In my case, God took the desire of pornography away from me and I never looked back–this was an immediate deliverance. Concerning self-pleasure, this would take years to break off me. These deliverance processes looked different and required various methods. Below will outline a deliverance prayer and process, but this should be contoured to your specific needs. The only one who can do that for you is Holy Spirit. Use this prayer and process as a guide, but ultimately, be led by *His* advice.

The Process of Deliverance from Lust

"When the righteous cry for help, the Lord hears and delivers them out of all their troubles." Psalm 34:17 (ESV)

"Then they cried to the Lord in their trouble, and he delivered them from their distress." Psalm 107:6 (ESV)

---

[2] Guzik, D. (2025). Enduring Word Bible Commentary 2 Samuel Chapter 12. https://enduringword.com/bible-commentary/2-samuel-12/

"And call upon me in the day of trouble; I will deliver you, and you shall glorify me." Psalm 50:15 (ESV)

"I sought the Lord, and he answered me and delivered me from all my fears." Psalm 34:4 (ESV)

"He said, "The Lord is my rock and my fortress and my deliverer.."" 2 Samuel 22:2 (ESV)

"In You, O Lord , I put my trust; Let me never be ashamed; Deliver me in Your righteousness. Bow down Your ear to me, Deliver me speedily; Be my rock of refuge, A fortress of defense to save me." Psalms 31:1-2 (NKJV)

The deliverance process is just that–a process. Yes, some people are able to pray a prayer of deliverance and be set free for the rest of their lives, but some people don't have praying grandmothers/ fathers or a father that has a covenant with the Lord ensuring your protection (2 Samuel 7:12-16 & 1 Kings 11:11-13). Some people have a history of witchcraft on their bloodline. When they sin, the reward for their sin is total destruction. If you are seeing the fruit of Exodus 20:5, and you are unsure if you are the 2nd or 4th generation, you might have to work a little harder to get the stubborn iniquity off your bloodline, especially if in the contract the next generations were promised to them during the acts of witchcraft. Whether you have a rich history of praying forefathers or a rich history of witchcraft, because of your humanity, there *will* be a process. There will be an unmasking of the delusions (Isaiah 66:4 and 2 Thessalonians 2:9-12) and reprobate mind (Romans 1:28) God allowed to come upon you. Coming out of idolatry, you will feel like you're waking from a deep sleep. Shame will try and sit on you, but understand that God says, "For your shame I will give you double honor..." (Isaiah 61:7-8) This means you must relinquish the shame of your past. God requires a trade; you cannot hide in shame yet expect His double honor. God even goes on to say, "Instead of confusion, you shall rejoice in your inheritance..." This is another exchange. When the scales of idolatry are dropped from your eyes, confusion of how you ended up there will try to take residence in your mind. This is when you choose if you will rent to confusion or allow inheritance to own your mind.

As you are delivered from lust, remember in God's love does He desire you to be free. I encourage you to work out your salvation with fear and trembling, but also, I encourage you to dive head-first into God's compassion and His love for you. Knowing that it is God's goodness that leads you to repentance (Romans 2:4). As you seek the Lord, He will answer you and deliver you from all that's not like Him. You are the 1 He has forsaken the 99 for, relish in being *His* 1. You are most worthy, in fact, you're to die for.

Below are 6 steps to being delivered from the covenant and curse of lust:

Please note:

- *This is including but not limited to. Be guided by Holy Spirit as you move forward with this process...*

- *Only pray to proceed with these six steps if you are truly ready for deliverance. PLEASE see page 1 of chapter 11, The Maintenance of Idolatry.*

1. **Repent.** "God, forgive me for all my sins, iniquities, and transgressions. I am deeply sorry for what I have done that has displeased you. If there are sin, iniquities, and transgressions I have done that I don't know about or remember, bring them to my memory so I won't do it again; so, I can have true repentance. God, give me a legal pardon in the realm of the spirit... I'm agreeing with my adversary [satan] quickly, whatever sin my adversary said I've/my bloodline has done...I break the legal right for these sins to

continue speaking against me/my bloodline through my repentance." (Leviticus 26:40-42).

2. **Renounce/Come Out of Agreement.** "God, I renounce, denounce and come out of agreement with any evil covenant that has been made through my sins, iniquities, and transgressions. God, show me the root to whatever has caused this evil covenant to come about and show me how to uproot even the residue of these curses out of my bloodline."

3. **Replace.** Ask God to replace the pain or whatever is happening with healing according to the stripes Jesus took on the cross (Isaiah 53:5-6). Look up the opposite of what is happening and speak the opposite or the antonym of what you're experiencing. e.g. replace generational poverty with generational wealth. Replace the sicknesses, diseases, early death, etc. with long life and good health. Replace lust with love and purity. Replace these generational curses with generational blessings (Matthew 12:43-45). "God, as I call for the replacing of these curses, help me to also remember that faith without works is dead. I speak these prayers by faith, teach me how to also work with Holy Spirit to do what it is you desire to see done in my life and bloodline, in the name of Jesus, amen!"

4. **Rule, Reign, Dominion.** "God, I have repented, renounced, and replaced these curses that have appeared in my life because of an evil covenant made by me or someone in my bloodline. Please give me and my bloodline a Holy Pardon in the realm of the spirit, instead of consequences. Pardon me so I don't reap the evil harvest of what was done. I speak the remission of sins over the evil covenant and curse. If it be your will, exonerate me and my bloodline, God. I give you rule, reign and dominion over me and my bloodline. God, have your way."

5. **Rebuke satan.** James 4:7 (NKJV) says, "Therefore submit to God. Resist the devil and he will flee from you." Matthew 4:10

(NKJV) says, "Then Jesus said to him, "Away with you, Satan! For it is written, 'You shall worship the Lord your God, and Him only you shall serve.'""

"Satan, you are now rebuked and I command you to flee from my life and my family's life. You have no access to attack us in this area. As we stay in a repentant heart posture, should you try and attack in this area, you are in high treason. I decree and declare no trace or residue of any curse will be on my life or my bloodline. I declare, me and my family are whole and healed. We will live and not die to declare the works of the Lord.

6. **Fasting and Praying.** Please Note* Some curses can be broken from simple identification & repentance, while some curses are stubborn and have been on a bloodline for ages and won't come out unless through prayer and biblical fasting (no food, only water for a period of time, designated by you and God). This is according to Matthew 17:21 "This 'kind' won't come out unless through prayer and fasting." (Kind=*genos*, kindred, offspring, nation, family, stock, tribe, race, etc..).

After these steps: create a plan for deliverance maintenance. Now, the real work begins; you must hold yourself accountable and find an accountability partner that will also hold you accountable. As you discover the root of lustful perversions, take a spiritual axe to them and destroy everything not like God. It's also important to remember that sin doesn't begin in action; sin begins in a thought. As you become a disciplined one (1 Corinthians 9:27), also become an investigator and find where your thoughts of lust begin on a daily—find your triggers. The average person has anywhere from 12,000-60,000 thoughts per day, every thought doesn't belong to you. Take your rightful authority and begin putting these thoughts on trial. As a judge, using your Biblical framework to persecute every thought or imagination that exalts itself against the knowledge of God, and bring into captivity every thought to the obedience of

Christ (2 Corinthians 10:5) sending them back to the pits of hell from whence they came. When those urges of sin come back, yes, rebuke Satan all day long (See #5), but also do the work to keep yourself far from temptation. How are you gate keeping your entrances (eyes, ears, mouth)? What doors and portals do you have open? Is your lifestyle conducive to one that has been delivered from lust? Do you hang around the same people that encouraged your lustful habits? Do you still visit the same lustful places, websites, etc.? Wear the same lustful clothes, listen to the same lustful music? Why are you continuing to watch that show, full of sexual innuendos? Prophetess Tiphani Montgomery once said, "Deliverance is for the desperate." The same desperation it took for you to get free is the same desperation it will take for you to remain free. Your house has been swept clean and put in order (Matthew 12:43-45), but ensure it is not *empty*. When satan sends his unclean spirit to prove your deliverance, be certain you've replaced your proclivity with something that will sustain your deliverance. Will satan find you fighting your tempting thoughts with disassociation, or will he find your house full of 10-20 scriptures you recite daily to keep your deliverance. If seven more spirits worse than lust enter the house (you), they're coming for permanent residence. More importantly, they're coming for blood, and this time they won't miss.

Idolatry of Money

"For the love of money is the root of all kinds of evil. And some people, craving money, have wandered from the true faith and pierced themselves with many sorrows." 1 Timothy 6:10 (NLT)

At this point based on the title of the chapter, you're probably thinking, *"Man, what isn't idolatry?"* To which I would respond, "I know, right," but reminder, it's the worship of that thing and your obedience to it that makes it idolatry. Even taking a deeper look into the scripture above, it's the "LOVE" of money that is the root of evil. Many people don't think they have made money an idol, their argument usually ends or begins with, "..because I need money to live and survive," to which I would acknowledge as valid, after my acknowledgement I would take you to Luke 9:3 and I would especially admonish you to study Matthew 6:24-34 so you to get a better revelation that if the God of the universe is telling *you* not to worry about what you'll eat or wear, why are you so concerned? No need to answer, I've already been convinced that your concern speaks to a deeper altar of idolatry. Yes, your love of money is about the clothes, what you'll eat, and taking care of yourself, but the real reason you check your banking apps more than your Bible app speaks to the worship in your heart. If it wasn't the clothes or food you had to concern yourself with, you would find another cover-up to excuse your adulterated love and desire for money.

The Spirit of Poverty

Now that I've convinced you or at the very least informed you there is such a thing as idolatry of money *and* that you might or might not be a participant, let me expose this spirit that works with it. It is one that occasionally serves as the foundation to the agreement or covenant made with the idolatry of money–the spirit of poverty. The spirit of poverty is sneaky. It usually dances with other spirits that crave the foreground. The spirit of poverty doesn't mind being in the shadows, it lets the attention seeking leviathan, jezebel, marine spirits or Absalom spirit have its way while it hides. The difference is, those spirits always leave traces of their identity behind, while the spirit of poverty offers a phantom scent. Hiding itself ever so slightly as to never be named as one of the culprits responsible for the damage in a believer's life. Leaving God's people being destroyed by ignorance because of the mindset that poverty is only about literal money, when really it is a paradigm, a way of life, a legacy. Poverty-stricken bloodlines waiting to hit it big, not knowing a lack of money is not even half of their problems. Poverty stricken bloodlines wondering why they have all the money in the world, yet their soul feels black and void. Masquerading as an attack to one demographic, while quietly really destroying both–the man with $2.50 and the man with 2.5 million dollars. The misconception is diabolical at best; but thank God for grace. Thank God He had enough mercy to put us on game. I've come to expose this spirit for what it is. No longer will we be blinded and misled. No longer will God's people be victims of this sneaky and sometimes dormant spirit molesting our bloodlines for generations. My prayer is that as you read, your deliverance will be hung on the shoulders of knowledge.

Some indicators a spirit of poverty is at work:

-   Selfishness & greed (Proverbs 11:24)

- Hoarding (Proverbs 28:27)

- Stubbornness, pride & shame (Proverbs 13:18)

- Laziness (Proverbs 10:4 & Proverbs 14:23)

- Insecurity (Proverbs 10:15)

- Scarcity (Proverb 6:11)

- Spiritual slumber (Proverbs 20:13)

- Impulsivity (Proverbs 21:5)

- Addiction (Proverbs 23:21)

- Insatiable (Proverbs 27:20)

- Sexual immorality (Proverbs 6:26)

- Procrastination (Proverbs 20:4)

*Take a moment and study these scriptures. As you study them, look them up in different translations and even seek to define the individual words as you feel led. After, take note to see if these things started with you or are generational.

Revelation 12:11

Here's a good place to share my testimony of how I broke the back of poverty off my life, thus breaking the idolatry of money as well. It all started in 2019 when I sought the Lord as to where I was supposed to move after graduating college. I was a military brat used to moving around the world, so I told God I wanted to be in *His* army, and He could move me where He pleased. In February of 2019, I sought His face and He told me where I would be moving, but the icing on this cake was that He wanted me to move without my car. North Carolina to Oklahoma; God wanted me to move 1,000 miles away without a vehicle. God told me He wanted me to *give* the car away. He also explained who to give it to as well as when–December of 2019. At the time, December was ten months away, but it felt like the next day. God said once I gave the car away, He would give me a car that was fully paid for, no car payment. He said it would just *come* to me and that it would be a miracle. The Lord warned me and said, "If you choose to be disobedient and take the car with you to Oklahoma, you won't make it there, it'll break down in the middle of the road." I reasoned that my parents bought me the car, it wasn't paid off, and everything else I could think of to not go to Oklahoma. In my process of coming to terms with the idea of moving to Oklahoma *and* giving away my car. The Lord gave me instructions to pray for my parent's hearts so they would agree to let me give away a car they purchased for me. In August I had a "press conference" to tell my family where I was moving to after graduation. Once the call ended, I asked my parents to stay on the line and told them the news. Thank God for parents that have a fear of the Lord and parents that also have the gift of giving. I've seen them give our last only to be blessed with more than what we gave immediately after—I was raised well! My dad said, "Well, who are we to stand the way of what God is telling you to do? I'll pay the car off before December, just in time for you to give it away." My mom agreed and encouraged me to trust the Lord to see me through. As I'm preparing the car I hear the Lord tell me to get an oil change and new tires. I pulled a Sarah in Genesis 18:11-15 and responded to the Lord with a laugh. To which He said, "The same way you want to receive this car is how I need you to give it. No car payment, delivered to her, oil changed, new tires– this is how I need you to give it away and watch me bless you with this in return." Two weeks before I'm preparing to give the car away in the last week of December I get into two accidents. With every accident I think, *I'm just not going to give this car away.* Immediately, I hear the Lord say, *"That's what the devil wants you to do. Do you know the level of faith this girl will have to see a move of God like this happen in her life. More than a blessing of a car, I want her faith. I need her bloodline's faith. I need them to know I am the God of all their needs; they don't need any other god. Not to mention your family, they need to see I am the God of miracles."* A week later I got into another accident that almost claimed my life and my mom's. At this point I'm ready to box the devil, but I knew the best way to get back at him was to give the car away. When I met the girl who I was giving my car to she kept saying, "Are you sure? Is this really happening? My family doesn't believe this is happening. They keep saying, "miracles like this don't happen anymore."" Confirmation that giving this car was about more than the car, it was about her faith and her family's faith, as well as the on-lookers to my obedience. I gave the car away, prayed over the young lady and caught my flight to Oklahoma on the same day. I expected to land with a car waiting for me, but it wouldn't be until 5 months of not having a car that I would finally receive one. During this time, I'm ubering to and from work, at least $20 a day–my savings is dwindling rapidly. I'm having to tuck in my pride and ask for rides. God humbled me so well that one day as I waited on a ride, I felt the urge to call a friend I used to give rides to in college and apologize to her. I said, "I'm so sorry I didn't give you rides with a cheerful heart. Every time you would ask for a ride I would oblige, but I would roll my eyes or have a negative thought. I'm experiencing that now and I am so sorry for being that way towards you." She was confused because I hid my disdain so well, but my heart was sorely convicted by the Lord; I was reaching a low place, but I know God wanted me there. To make matters more complicated, this is also when the Lord told me to stop asking my mom for money and letting my parents pay my rent. Three months in Oklahoma as a teacher and I have more bills than money. God said, "If your mom asks to pay your rent this month, I need you to tell her, "NO"". The Lord went on to say, "You trust in your parents and friends to provide for you better than I can. I won't compete as your provider, you are not to *ask* for money, but if someone sends or offers it, you can accept." I didn't realize my idolatry was so deep in-to people that I had them shelved as lowercase "g" god's my heart. I had made men my Jireh and I was wrong. As God would have it, the next day my mom asked to pay my rent, there was eternity in my pause. Two worlds fought within me, to be or not to be disobe-dient. As the, "no" left my lips a fear of the unknown mixed with a serenity of the God I serve overcame me. At that moment, as I made a conscious choice to put Him in His rightful place as Jireh, like clockwork, random refund checks showed up in the mail. I re-ceived money from family and friends saying I was on their mind. Some days I would have the money to get to work, but none to get home, other teachers would randomly come by and ask if I needed a ride. Sometimes stranded at the school praying for Jireh to show up, someone would call me and say, "I never do this, but God told me to send you some money, so I'm sending it now." Proving God's prophecy from February the previous year that if I went to Oklaho-ma He would send the Ravens to take care of me like He did Elijah. Birds known to never sow, nor reap would be taking care of me. With my savings on E, God was faithful to provide everything I needed. That's when the pandemic hits and the world shut down. I didn't need money to get to work, but a new problem arose. I would be starting graduate school in the summer, and I would need a way to get to and from classes. Two months before I got a car, my dad came to visit for my birthday, and he asked me if I wanted him to buy me a car. With every question I felt my faith growing weaker, but every time my dad or my mom asked, I recited what God said to me "As you give your car, you will receive one in the same way. No car payment, delivered to you, oil changed, new tires and more." In unexplainable Godly wisdom, I had an inkling that wasn't supposed to come from my parents. The pressure from my parents to buy me a car was coupled with my brother offering up a 16 passenger van he was willing to drive over from Colorado. While I appreciated the sentiment, for obvious reasons I prayed harder asking God for an ETA on my miracle as to avoid driving a van fit for a church choir. On my dad's last day in town, I made an inward vow that if he asked to buy me a car again, I would say yes. You guessed it, he didn't ask again, he didn't even bring up the subject. Fast forward to May, two days before I got the call I was getting a car, I was in despair. Classes would start soon and I felt forsaken. I have a real talk with God about my disappointment, but I end the talk with thanksgiving because I don't know Him to be a liar. I go on with my day fighting hopelessness with joy and faith. On the day I got the news I would be getting a car; I was on the phone with a (at the time) sorority sister/ friend from college. I knew her only as a line sister, but in the months after I graduated, I began to know her as a sister in Christ. Ultimately, this line sister and I would seek God's face for truth and denounce the sorority together, but I'll save that for another testimony. In the middle of me explaining my woes to her, specifically that I start school in exactly one month and needed a car, she abruptly stopped me and began to explain exactly how she was getting closer to God. She began to explain how a few months ago she couldn't discern her voice or the enemy's from the voice of God, but now she can. That's when she says, "God told me to give you my car back in December and a few days ago He told me again, this time with an urgency, He said I need to have it delivered to you in exactly one month. He told me this in December, but I just didn't know if it was God or my flesh. Now with this confirmation of you starting school in a month I know it was God; He has not let me rest until I began making the arrangements to give you this car." At this point my jaw is on the ground in disbelief. I knew I would be getting a free car; I just didn't know it would feel like this. I always imagined I would be on the set of the Price is Right or Oprah, so this scenario never crossed my mind. As we were making the arrangements for the car to be *delivered* to me free of charge, she highlighted that the car was paid off, with a recent oil change, new windshield wipers and new tires.

Further in awe because minus the new windshield wipers, that's exactly how I gave my old car away. A few days before class begins, my brand new, paid-off car arrives at my apartment with the title, with less miles on it than the car I gave away, and a more current year and a nicer model. In addition, God provided someone to sow into me to get my tags and car registration. It wouldn't be until a few months later I recount this testimony with God that He would tell me, "Well done, Kayla. You've broken the back of poverty by *giving* your car away. You waited well for five months and in those five months I killed off pride and placed humility within you. In those five months, your empathy and compassion increased and now I can use you for greater things. In five months, you've placed me on my rightful throne as your Jehovah Jireh; now you finally understand, people could never take care of you the way I do. Thank you for trusting me and thank you for being my example in the Earth of Crazy Faith." I've had that car for some years now, but I know it's not mine. One day soon I'll be transferring the title to someone else and riding in a new car that God has given me. The true reward for breaking the spirit of poverty and destroying the idolatry of money is to become a serial sower. The more I give, I remind the spirit of poverty, "This bloodline is spoken for. You cannot have my family, and you cannot have my children. The curse is broken."

The Compromise for Money

"But I have a few things against you, because you have there those who hold the doctrine of Balaam, who taught Balak to put a stumbling block before the children of Israel, to eat things sacrificed to idols, and to commit sexual immorality. Thus you also have those who hold the doctrine of the Nicolaitans, which thing I hate. Repent, or else I will come to you quickly and will fight against them with the sword of My mouth." Revelation 2:14-16 NKJV)

Can You Be Bought for a Price?

In the book of Numbers 22-24, it follows a story about a compromised prophet–Prophet Balaam. Balaam had gotten a name in the land of being one who when he spoke, those who were blessed were indeed blessed and those who were cursed were indeed cursed. He was asked by Balak, king of the Moabites to curse the children of Israel because he heard about the great things their God did to the Egyptians and was sore afraid his people would be next. While Balaam was compromised by the dollar, He still feared the Lord and knew enough that he couldn't curse a people unless God willed him to. Balaam was like that teenager that incessantly begs to do something foolish and when the parent has had enough, obliged, yet is filled with anger because they know what lies ahead. Long story short, every time Balaam goes to seek God's voice in hopes to complete his job and curse the children of Israel, God bestows a blessing upon them. His contracted employer (Balak) gets upset and Balaam goes on his way. *Please read the chapters for yourself.

I imagine Balaam didn't start out to be a compromised prophet/ diviner. Judging by his fear of the Lord, he grew up rightly and knew not to cross the God who parted the red sea then closed it up on His enemies. The idolatry of money, or the love, obedience and worship he had towards money ultimately led to his demise (Numbers 31:8-16). A CEO arrested for embezzlement probably never set out to misappropriate funds; prostitutes never start out to sell their bodies; politicians don't start off crooked (most of them anyway). It starts off with little compromises that lead to grave sins. Studying this particular situation with Balaam, the first compromise was when he didn't immediately turn the Moabite representatives away. This led to him begging God to travel with them to their city multiple times, then the sacrifices, etc. All the devil needs is to plant a seed.

What Seeds of Compromise Have You Been Making

This story in Numbers is what the Lord uses a lot to warn me against such practices as I ascend to entrepreneurship. The Lord gave me a business (Books By KJF, LLC) back in 2021 and a prayer ministry (Dancing Wives Prayer Ministry) in 2023. In 2023 I was blessed through various streams of income and rather than blow it on frivolous things, I decided to take that money and invest it in my business and my ministry. The business and ministry were doing well, but I still begged God for a personal increase. Often there were times when my ministry and business had income and I did not. That's when I heard the Lord say:

"Kayla, I can't bless your ministry and business like I want to right now because your personal finances couldn't handle it." Initially confused, God went on to say, "You've always done very well stewarding the money I give you for other people. If I give you $1,000 and tell you $900 of that is for other people you give it, but my concern is what you do with your $100. You blow your $100 in minutes, sometimes you've spent it before you've received it. I cannot bless what you have yet to steward. If I bless your business and your ministry with income, while your personal accounts are dry, can you tell me you wouldn't be tempted to borrow money from the business or ministry with the thought process, "I'll put it back the next time I get paid." Can you honestly say, you wouldn't be tempted? So, Kayla I cannot bless your ministry and business in financially explosive ways because I cannot bless you personally, until you steward well over the little, I have given you."

During these times God was teaching me about the spirit of compromise. The Lord began and truthfully still is walking with me as I practice discipline in my personal finances. I sow like it's going out of style, but the money set aside for me hates to see a shoe sale. My dad would say, "Kayla you've got a hole in your pocket," as I asked for money every week in high school. In my receptivity to

God's assistance with my budgets, I've done well with keeping a budget, because even though it hasn't been much to manage on a teacher's salary, I'm trying to live out Matthew 25:21 reward and hear those famous words, "His lord said to him, 'Well *done*, good and faithful servant; you were faithful over a few things, I will make you ruler over many things. Enter into the joy of your lord." He's been teaching me to be a good steward and all-around businesswoman. Warning me against co-mingling of accounts and funds, while also giving me opportunities to show him I can be ruler over many things. I'm currently training my brain to instinctively decide that integrity comes first: even if that means a fee must be incurred or if I must inconveniently go to the bank to make transfers. To be faithful over a few and one day ruler over much requires sacrifice and requires tedious habits. Yes, the IRS/FBI/XYZ can be a scary authority figure and that's a reason to keep things upright, but God is the one who elevates. God is the one who I must first answer to and whoa unto the "Christian" business owner that falls into the hands of a living God by cutting corners in their business and ministry's finances. When those convictions begin to wane and that reprobate mind begins to form…a Judas fall is imminent.

Idolatry of Money Blinds Your Discernment

"After this Jehoshaphat king of Judah allied himself with Ahaziah king of Israel, who acted very wickedly. And he allied himself with him to make ships to go to Tarshish, and they made the ships in Ezion Geber. But Eliezer the son of Dodavah of Mareshah prophesied against Jehoshaphat, saying, "Because you have allied yourself with Ahaziah, the LORD has destroyed your works." Then the ships were wrecked, so that they were not able to go to Tarshish."
2 Chronicles 20:35-37 (NKJV)

We've seen this too many times: a woman or a man trapped in a marriage with a person simply because of the person's wealth. A person stuck at a job they hate or that's killing them–simply because it paid well. A young kid offered to make some extra money only to look up months or years later selling drugs or other illegal items because of the fast money. All these scenarios end the same way, in destruction (Proverbs 14:12). The root of this destruction was their idolatry or worship of money. Losing sight of who they were coming into agreement with by accepting the money. 2 Chronicles 20:35-37 is proof who you are allied with or in covenant agreement with can be the cause of your demise.

You might be wondering, how does this happen; at the very least, *how do I prevent it from happening to me*. In 2 Chronicles 20:32-33, we see that while Jehoshaphat did what was right in the sight of the Lord, the problem was he had not taken down the "High Places" or the "Places of worship to other gods."

"And he walked in the way of his father Asa, and did not turn aside from it, doing what was right in the sight of the Lord. Nevertheless the high places were not taken away, for as yet the people had not directed their hearts to the God of their fathers." 2 Chronicles 20:32-33

Ask yourself, what high places have you yet to renounce and remove from God's throne. These high places will be the very thing that blindly leads you into a partnership with satan himself. Psalms 115:5-8 (NKJV) describes it best, *"'They have mouths, but they do not speak; Eyes they have, but they do not see; Their idols are silver and gold, The work of men's hands. They have ears, but they do not hear; Noses they have, but they do not smell; They have hands, but they do not handle; Feet they have, but they do not walk; Nor do they mutter through their throat. Those who make them are like them; So is everyone who trusts in them."* A lot of people, like their idols, find themselves with mouths, but are silent so as not to disrupt their flow of money. With eyes, but unable to see the evil attached to the currency they receive. Worshiping the gift and not the gift giver. Giving God's glory to the man that handed them the check. With ears, but they cannot hear the Holy Spirit telling them to run because His voice has been quenched time and time again. Noses, but they cannot smell foul play of idol worship in the air. Hands, but they use their hands to glorify themselves, so all the works of their hands are destroyed. Feet, but the order of their steps divinely set before them to walk in righteousness, they've refused. When asked by the Lord above *all* lords to stand before Him like a man to explain themselves, unlike Job in Job 38:3 they had a lump in their throats. To seal this fate, Isaiah 66:17 (NIV) offers insight on their reward for idolatry, *"Those who consecrate and purify themselves to go into the gardens, following [their idol] one who is among those who eat the flesh of pigs, rats and other unclean things—they will meet their end together with the one they follow," declares the Lord."* Reason number 336 as to why I fear the Lord: He's declared to bury us amongst our idols, lest we repent.

Revelation 12:11

I knew a girl from high school. She and her baby fell into some tough times and I wanted to give them some money. Before I sent the message, asking for her information to send the money, I heard Holy Spirit's voice clearly tell me not to give His money to that girl. I just knew it was the devil, so I persisted in proofreading the message to send. I heard Him again. I've never heard God's audible voice, but I hear Him in my thoughts; thoughts that I know could never be mine. When I don't respond to Holy Spirit or I'm preparing a statement to quench Him, the thought He gave me almost begins to pound in the bounds of my thought process. This is when conviction kicks in, the pounding tap dances on my conviction nerve until I cannot handle the pounding of disobedience, which ends in me acknowledging or obliging the Holy Spirit in His request. My convictions are so heavy, they tend to torment me until I'm obedient. Later I'll share how ignoring my convictions and being disobedient almost led me to suicide. Nonetheless, back to the testimony. As the pounding commenced, I heard Holy Spirit explaining to me (an explanation He granted me in His mercy, because He didn't have to explain Himself) that I had no idea what I was joining or coming into agreement with by sending her money. He went on to explain that in her rebellion to serve satan is what caused her to find despair as her fate. This is when He began to warn me about my financial choices and partnerships, especially as I graduate to the place where I'll find that my money knows no limitation. Holy Spirit began to tell me to practice saying "no." Educating me on the differences between "Good causes vs. God causes." He explained that there would be situations where it makes no sense *not* to sow, but God will say no and I will need to have the courage to look the person (family, friend or foe) in the eye and tell them "no, period." Holy Spirit also went on to say, "Man looks at the outward appearance, but I look at the heart" (1 Samuel 16:7). What you can't see are the soul ties and demonic covenant this person is tied up in that you will soon reap, should you sow. What you cannot see is that when you sow where I have not granted, that person might look to make you their Jehovah Jireh and I am jealous over my children. What you cannot see is that their wages of sin is death, yet in my mercy I'm simply allowing the devourer to *financially* kill them instead of literally. This is when I began to declare myself a Kingdom financier and a glory carrier of wealth. Vowing to only finance the things of *God's* kingdom here on Earth. This doesn't come without sacrifice. The Lord began to tell me what restaurants I could no longer eat at because of their agreements, clothes I could no longer wear, and businesses I needed to stop supporting. To this day, to resist these things can be difficult, but what a shame it would be to walk upright in all my ways, and like Jehoshaphat, because of the high places in my heart, lose it all due to a partnership with the wrong person/people.

What is the Exchange of Money Costing You?

In 2 Kings chapter five, Gehazi took money from Naaman and as a result, Elisha pronounced the same disease Naaman was cured from to be brought to not only Gehazi, but to his descendants forever.

"He went in and stood before his master, and Elisha said to him, "Where have you been, Gehazi?" And he said, "Your servant went nowhere." But he said to him, "Did not my heart go when the man turned from his chariot to meet you? Was it a time to accept money and garments, olive orchards and vineyards, sheep and oxen, male servants and female servants? Therefore the leprosy of Naaman shall cling to you and to your descendants forever." So he went out from his presence a leper, like snow." 2 Kings 5:25-27 (NLT)

*Examine your partnerships. Financially and in other areas as Holy Spirit leads. If they are evil partnerships renounce, denounce and come out of agreement immediately.

Pray this prayer:

Dear God, you said that we, your people, are destroyed because we lack knowledge. You said we perish because of our ignorance. God, I have the overwhelming sense I've been pershing because of my ignorance. In many places, but specifically financially. God, I'm asking in the authority of Jesus Christ that you forgive me for my sins, forgive me for my comfortability with being ignorant. I stand here on behalf of my bloodline as the repairer of broken walls concerning the financial abundance you've promised as our inheritance to be your children. God, forgive us for being idolatrous fools and loving money more than we love you. Forgive us for thinking that we could be Jireh or looking for Jireh from every other person but you. Let Heaven and Earth record that this day, I renounce the idol of money out of my heart. Out of the heart of my bloodline. I replace our love of money with the love of you, our Father. God, I put you back in your rightful place in our hearts and I crown you King–have rule, reign, and dominion over us. Father as I walk out this deliverance and in faith as I believe my family to also be delivered, strengthen us to say no to a love for money. Help us when we are faced with an opportunity to choose money in the form of a partnership over you. Holy Spirit, through Prophet Isaiah you wrote, "And your ears shall hear a word behind you, saying, "This is the way, walk in it," when you turn to the right or when you turn to the left." (Isaiah 30:21, (NKJV)). Guide my bloodline as we make decisions. Help us to not only listen for your voice, but to be obedient to your voice as well. Finally, Jehovah Jireh restores to us the resources and wealth that is due us. Father what has been stolen, according to Proverbs 6:31, the thief has been caught, I command our seven-fold + blessing to manifest now. All that has been withheld, I command the latter and the former rain to come down now. I command the Earth to open and to yield my bloodline our fruit that we are due. I command the wealth of the wicked to be transferred to the righteousness of my bloodline, now. God, as you do this, help us to be good stewards over this new season of financial resources and blessings. Help us to give you your tithe and beyond. Show us practically how to budget and save. Jehovah Sabaoth, we need your strategy. Thank you, God, for giving us this day and all days, our daily bread. In Jesus' matchless name, amen.

Generational Idolatry of Money

If we could pick our families, I can imagine about half of this world would choose differently. Those who identify as the gap standers (Ezekiel 22:30) or the repairers of the breach, (Isaiah 58:12) I know the burden it is to repent on behalf of a bloodline. To turn from wicked ways on behalf of a bloodline yet have people (spirits) from that same bloodline turn on you, criticize you, and refuse to change. The backlash and retaliation from the iniquity workers on a bloodline alone are enough to make a person want to give up, still we press towards the mark. While we could never know what it took for Jesus to die on that cross, I imagine repenting on behalf of a bloodline that wants to stay in Egypt is a distant close. I believe Abraham, Moses, Caleb, and Joshua could tell us a little bit about that. I've digressed; chances are, your idolatry of money didn't start with you–it probably started generations ago. The good news? It's going to end with you. Continue to be the bloodline repairer. I know it's not easy, but God will be faithful to honor your commitment to your bloodline, more important your commitment to act as a reconciliation bridge from God to your family. If you haven't heard it from anyone else, let me be the first to congratulate you.

Congratulations, your bloodline will never be financially the same because of your allegiance to God! Well done, bloodline repairer. Continue to press towards the mark!

Idolatry of Emotions

"But understand this, that in the last days dangerous times [of great stress and trouble] will come [difficult days that will be hard to bear]. For people will be lovers of self [narcissistic, self-focused], lovers of money [impelled by greed], boastful, arrogant, revilers, disobedient to parents, ungrateful, unholy and profane, [and they will be] unloving [devoid of natural human affection, calloused and inhumane], irreconcilable, malicious gossips, devoid of self-control [intemperate, immoral], brutal, haters of good, traitors, reckless, conceited, lovers of [sensual] pleasure rather than lovers of God, holding to a form of [outward] godliness (religion), although they have denied its power [for their conduct nullifies their claim of faith]. Avoid such people and keep far away from them."
2 Timothy 3:1-5 (AMP)

What is Emotional Idolatry

We are taught emotions are a bad thing, and this couldn't be further from the intended creative design. God, our designer doesn't have a problem with our emotions; He has emotions as well. God has a problem when we experience our emotions outside of Him. When we take our emotions—the things He has placed on the inside of us for our good and use them to sin against *Him*. The Bible is clear in Ephesians 4:26 when it talks about being angry, yet not sinning, nor letting the sun go down on our anger. The actual emotion was never the problem, it's what happens as a manifested result of the emotion. Because an idol is anything we love more than our obedience to God or our worship of something or someone over God; emotional idolatry is when you prioritize or are obedient to your emotions before you are to the will of God. If you have a greater obedience to how you feel in the moment than you do to the mandate in your life, you are in idolatry. Oftentimes we use our emotions as an excuse to be disobedient to God. For example, if God told you to do something weighty and/or scary like write a book. Because life is constantly life-ing, while God is always God-ing, He probably will ask you to write this book in one of the saddest seasons of your life. Emotional idolatry is choosing not to write the book because you feel sadness in this season, thus you are choosing to live in that emotion. Making a cognitive decision to be more obedient to your emotion, than to God. Refusing the truth of God, that He is good, despite all circumstances, only to believe the lie of your emotions. In addition to believing the lie, also choosing to be faithful and worship the lie over God–there is the idolatry that is smoke in God's nostrils. A Biblical example of the opportunity for emotional idolatry is with Samuel. In 1 Samuel 16 when God told Samuel to stop crying over Saul, emotional idolatry would have been evident if Samuel would have continued to lament and not complete his assignment because he was so sad (Study 1 Samuel 16). Instead, Samuel dried his tears and went about his next assignment. In this moment he showed us, most importantly God, that he was not a slave to his emotions.

You might even be one of God's children that is often begging to be used by Him, but transparently, He cannot trust you because you're finicky; you're a liability to the Kingdom of God. It's not because you *have* emotions, but it's because those emotions are not subject to the control of the authority of Jesus Christ placed on the inside of you. Throughout the haze of emotional idolatry, your truth becomes whatever anger or happiness says about you, that day, or in that moment rather than the truth of God found in His word. An indication you're living with emotional idolatry is when God tells you to do something and because you don't feel like it, you don't do it. Your fleeting and temporary feelings just argued a case against the one and true living God. While it looks like you won, be not deceived, you are in a losing battle. Should you continue on this path, death is imminent (Romans 6:23).

Okay, maybe that last part was harsh, but it's true. The wages of our sin *is* death. God mentions idolatry too often in the Bible for us to dismiss how much it truly hurts and upsets Him when we place another god or thing before Him. Maybe it's not an immediate drop-dead death like Ananias and Sapphira in Acts 5, but it could be a slow, painful, spiritual death. It could also be a financial death, mental death, etc. The scripture as it's read and interpreted is alive, quick, and powerful, sharper than a two-edged sword (Hebrews 4:12). Lest you repent, you will have your day in the courts of Heaven. Let us not abuse His grace in thinking we are absolved from being paid a wage of death because of the blood of Jesus Christ. We must reframe our thinking to compute that the blood was shed for the *remission* of our sins, as we *ask* God for forgiveness that was freely given to us when Jesus' blood hit that pavement, ushering us into the new covenant. When John the Baptist advised us to, "Repent, for the Kingdom of Heaven is at hand" (Matthew 3:2 (NKJV)), He wasn't saying it to sound important, it was instruction, a warning and mercy. Saul was paid his wage of a mental death because of his unrepentant disobedience. God in His mercy allowed him to rule for 40 additional years–slowly dying inside from mental torment. In Revelation 2:20-21, God reminds the Corrupt Church how disgusted He was that they tolerated that woman Jezebel, and God insisted that He gave her time to repent, yet she was unwilling. God isn't asking for much, He simply wants us to repent (Revelation 2:1-7) and turn back to our first love, *Him.*

As we've read above, emotions are not a bad thing. If you have heard your whole life how emotional you are and this statement has been used against you, I want to apologize. You are feeling the exact feelings God has designed for you. To have emotions makes you human, it makes you His image bearer. Again, it's simply the manifestation of those emotions outside of the presence and control of God that causes us to sin, removing us further from God's image and leading us into emotional idolatry. As I offer a God-given solution and an avenue of escape from emotional idolatry, I want to invite you to think of all the lives saved, problems solved, addictions healed, and people whole if our emotions were Godly regulated. It's also important to trace any vices and addictions, such as, but not limited to alcohol, drug, sex, etc. to a lack of emotional regulation. If our emotions were subject to the Holy Spirit that is housed within us, we would see such an improvement in the life of believers and nonbelievers alike.

Examples of Emotions in the Bible

A prerequisite to understanding the depth and harm of emotional idolatry is to first identify the most common, yet basic emotions (emotions are very nuanced and complex). As well as the places where these emotions are sighted in the Bible: sadness, happiness, fear, anger, surprise and disgust.

Sadness- *a* feeling or showing sorrow; unhappy.

"But to Hannah he would give a double portion, for he loved Hannah, although the Lord had closed her womb. And her rival also provoked her severely, to make her miserable, because the Lord had closed her womb. So it was, year by year, when she went up to the house of the Lord, that she provoked her; therefore she wept and did not eat." 1 Samuel 1: 5-7 (NKJV)

Hannah's circumstances produced this great anguish. It was a disgrace for a woman in this time to not have children. In the text we see not only did Hannah have emotions, but she also emoted in a way that got someone's attention. Before she did that, she made a wager with God. She leveraged, on faith. She knew God needed a judge and she wanted a son. She made a deal with God and God obliged. Proof of this is how in one season God used Eli to partner his faith with Hannah to conceive and in the next, God used him to train up her child. If we continue in the chapter, when Hannah left God's presence, she left her emotions at God's feet. Oftentimes, when we are in a bitter weep like Hannah, we get up from the presence of God before He can strip us of the seed of sin planted within the emotion–we don't place it completely at His feet. We can learn a lot from Hannah's strategy here because before the year was out, Hannah conceived and had in her arms the child she prayed for.

When David and his men reached Ziklag, they found it destroyed by fire and their wives and sons and daughters taken captive. So David and his men wept aloud until they had no strength left to weep. David's two wives had been captured—Ahinoam of Jezreel and Abigail, the widow of Nabal of Carmel. David was greatly distressed because the men were talking of stoning him; each one was bitter in spirit because of his sons and daughters. But David found strength in the Lord his God. 1 Samuel 30:3-6 (NIV)

David will always be my favorite example of emotional regulation in the Lord. He never emoted outside the presence of God. He took all his emotions to the Lord and would leave strengthened with an unexplainable peace. David was not perfect, but when he did slip up, his heart posture always directed him back to the presence of God for correction. Nonetheless, he is a great example of experiencing the emotions of life with the Lord. Like David, in your emotional dysregulation, may you always find your strength in the Lord and allow Him to regulate you continuously.

Happiness- the state of being happy which is the feeling or showing pleasure or contentment.

"And David danced before the Lord with all his might, clad in a linen ephod [a priest's upper garment]." 2 Samuel 6:14 (NKJV)

In this scripture we see David showing so much contentment in the Lord as he danced in a manner that was not befitting a king, but a servant. David's happiness was expressed through dance, the only thing about the emotion of happiness is, it is fleeting. People often equate being happy to happiness. You can be in a loving relationship, very content, very happy, but not experience happiness all the time. We cannot rethink our relationship every time we feel unhappy; realize you had an unhappy emotion, but you are not unhappy. This emotion of happiness must always be submitted to the Lord because as the world's barometer of happiness shifts with the Earth's tectonic plates, God's barometer of joy never changes (John 15:11). Another reason this emotion must be submitted to the Lord is because in 2 Samuel 6:14 David *felt* happiness and danced before the Lord, but in Psalms 103, David had to *command* his soul to bless the Lord, when he *felt* sadness. We live in a time where people have to "feel" happiness in order to praise the Lord. This is not realistic, nor is this acceptable to a *good* God. Because this emotion of happiness is fleeting, if we waited until we felt happiness in this imperfect world to praise, our praise would always and consistently be few and far between.

Challenge: The next time something disappointing happens and you don't *feel* happiness, I encourage you to praise the Lord. Offer up a sacrifice of praise (Hebrews 13:15) to the Lord in efforts to exchange the spirit of heaviness for the garment of praise (Isaiah 61:3). While always maintaining the knowledge that the temporary emotion of happiness will never be a match to the permanent soul level contentment of joy. Joy that God provides and will never take away.

Fear-an unpleasant emotion caused by the belief that someone or something is dangerous, to cause pain, or a threat.

"For we have heard how the Lord dried up the water of the Red Sea for you when you came out of Egypt, and what you did to the two kings of the Amorites who were on the other side of the Jordan, Sihon and Og, whom you utterly destroyed. And as soon as we heard these things, our hearts melted; neither did there remain any more courage in anyone because of you, for the Lord your God, He is God in heaven above and on earth beneath." Joshua 2:10-11 (NKJV)

"Men's hearts failing them from fear and the expectation of those things which are coming on the earth, for the powers of the heavens will be shaken." Luke 21:26 (NKJV)

Imagine your heart melting or failing you because of fear? Some of us don't have to imagine because it happens all the time. The spirit and the emotion of fear grips us with both hands and demands our heart as their prize. Fear that has likely traveled through the bloodline and refuses to let you or the next generation go without a fight. Proof of this can be found in Genesis 12:12 when Abram lied to the king about his wife Sarai and again when his son, Issac did the exact same thing with his wife Rebecca. Their common sin, fear. Their natural emotion to fear losing their lives on account of their beautiful wives was something that God could have helped them with; however, they allowed the spirit of fear to enter in their hearts, and in doing so, they sinned against God.

"Do not be afraid of them, for I am with you and will rescue you," declares the Lord. "Get yourself ready! Stand up and say to them whatever I command you. Do not be terrified by them, or I will terrify you before them." Jeremiah 1:8, 17 (NIV)

Jeremiah, a young prophet, had every right to be afraid; but, as he took his natural emotion of fear to the Lord, he was able to be reassured by the Lord. Due to the weight of Jeremiah's calling, the Lord also needed to remind Jeremiah that his fear or reverence only belonged to Him. The great and terrible God is the only one we should fear (Nehemiah 1:5).

Anger- a strong feeling of annoyance, displeasure, or hostility.

"...but on Cain and his offering he did not look with favor. So Cain was very angry, and his face was downcast/ Then the Lord said to Cain, "Why are you angry? Why is your face downcast? If you do what is right, will you not be accepted? But if you do not do what is right, sin is crouching at your door; it desires to have you, but you must rule over it." Now Cain said to his brother Abel, "Let's go out to the field." While they were in the field, Cain attacked his brother Abel and killed him." Genesis 4:5-8 (NKJV)

Cain's emotion of anger was not the problem; it was the sin committed because of his emotion. This anger, like many of ours, is so misplaced. This emotion of anger came from a lack of personal accountability. Abel did what the Lord asked Him and as a result became blessed; Cain did not. Cain didn't obey the Lord and instead of admitting that, he murdered his brother, the one who did heed the Lord's instructions. This should also give insight into what emotions that are not Godly regulated produce. What started as a natural emotion of anger ended in a murder scene and a curse. This is indicative of so many in our prison systems now. Their natural emotion, unsubmitted to God, resulted in the rest of their life behind bars and behind them a grieving family of their victim(s). When Cain was in the presence of God as he was being questioned, this is where he could have deposited anger at God's feet, yet he left God's presence even angrier. As mentioned earlier, the opposite is true with Hannah, she was able to wash off the emotion of sadness at God's feet. Had Cain been honest with God about his emotions and surrendered them to God what alternative outcomes would have taken place?

Surprise-an unexpected or astonishing event, fact, or thing.

"And as Peter knocked at the door of the gate, a girl named Rhoda came to answer. When she recognized Peter's voice, because of her gladness she did not open the gate, but ran in and announced that Peter stood before the gate. But they said to her, "You are beside yourself!" Yet she kept insisting that it was so. So they said, "It is his angel." Now Peter continued knocking; and when they opened the door and saw him, they were astonished." Acts 12: 13-16 (NKJV)

With surprise being a mostly positive emotion, in our pride we might think we don't need to submit this to the throne of grace to be Godly regulated, but that is inaccurate. The enemy walks around like a roaring lion seeking who he may (1 Peter 5:8), so if there's the slightest chance, he can take your emotion of surprise and pervert it, he will. Could the sin in these prayer warriors' heart's be that they were surprised that God did the very thing they were praying for (Mark 11:24)? They were willing to spend all night in a prayer meeting with no real expectation of a miracle. Or maybe they were simply ignorant to the effectiveness of their prayers. Their reflective question should be, "Why were we so surprised God did what He said He was going to do in freeing Peter? Do we not believe in the power of God? Do we not have faith?" Regardless, every emotion is worth a reflective therapy session with Holy Spirit, whether it is a perceived positive emotion or a negative one.

Disgust-a feeling of revulsion or strong disapproval aroused by something unpleasant or offensive.

"The next day as they were leaving Bethany, Jesus was hungry. Seeing in the distance a fig tree in leaf, he went to find out if it had any fruit. When he reached it, he found nothing but leaves, because it was not the season for figs. Then he said to the tree, "May no one ever eat fruit from you again." And his disciples heard him say it.

On reaching Jerusalem, Jesus entered the temple courts and began driving out those who were buying and selling there. He overturned the tables of the money changers and the benches of those selling doves and would not allow anyone to carry merchandise through the temple courts. And as he taught them, he said, "Is it not written: 'My house will be called a house of prayer for all nations'? But you have made it a den of robbers." Mark 11:12-17 (NIV)

Do you know how hungry Jesus had to be to curse a fig tree? Yes, of course there is a principle here, nonetheless, this is the true comedy of the Bible! This shows us that Jesus had emotions as well, Hebrews 4:14-16 tells us we have a savior that experienced everything we did, yet He did not sin. Everything Jesus did was to bring order and to prepare a people for his death and resurrection–as it was written. If a regular person were to enter the temple flipping chairs and tables with a righteous indignation, while they would have been justified, this would have been accounted to them as a sin. Yet when our Lord and savior, Jesus Christ did it, He was operating in the highest apostolic anointing in bringing order to what needed Heavenly alignment.

Example of a Downfall Because of Lack of Emotional Regulation:

In Exodus 2, Moses was an angry man (Exodus 2:12) and he feared (Exodus 2:14). Underneath Moses' show of anger was disappointment; he was disappointed with the maltreatment of God's people in Egypt, but the only way he knew how to express his disappointment, frustration and helplessness was through anger. Moses is also a prime example of time not healing all or any wounds. Moses isolated himself for 40 years, yet he didn't heal the disappointment manifested into anger he experienced when he was in Egypt–Moses simply dissociated. His encounter at Kadesh when he struck the rock twice, speaks to the emotional decisions Moses occasionally made. Disappointment manifested as anger caused him to kill a man in Egypt and as leader of all Israelites, this misman-agement of emotions eventually led him to dishonor God in the face of all of Israel, keeping him out of the promised land.

Some additional examples in the Bible of those who were at war with their own emotions are:

- Aaron: was jealous.

- Saul: was led by the emotions of others (people pleaser).

- Elijah: was scared into isolation by Jezebel, which led to depression.

- Elijah: was a man of "like" passions (passions like you and I). James 5:17

Now the greatest example of them all–you. Are your emotions often guiding you down erroneous paths? Today is a great day to wage war on the mismanagement of emotions.

God Has Emotions Just Like Us

God saw that human evil was out of control. People thought evil, imagined evil—evil, evil, evil from morning to night. God was sorry *that he had made the human race in the first place; it broke his heart. God said, "I'll get rid of my ruined creation, make a clean sweep: people, animals, snakes and bugs, birds—the works. I'm sorry I made them." Genesis 6:5-7 (MSG)*

When Jesus saw her weeping, and the Jews who had come along with her also weeping, he was deeply moved in spirit and troubled. "Where have you laid him?" he asked. "Come and see, Lord," they replied. Jesus wept. Then the Jews said, "See how he loved him!" John 11:33-36 (NIV)

"Then the word of the Lord came to Samuel, saying, "I regret that I made Saul king, for he has turned away from following Me

and has not carried out My commands." Samuel was angry [over Saul's failure] and he cried out to the Lord all night." 1 Samuel 15:10-11 (AMP)

The good news is deliverance through knowledge can be yours to-day:

"A hypocrite with his mouth destroyeth his neighbour: but through knowledge shall the just be delivered." Proverbs 11:9 (KJV)

With the Holy Spirit, reflect on any strong emotions you've experienced lately or have been experiencing for life. If none come to mind, ask Holy Spirit these questions and await His answer:

What emotions do I experience daily?

Am I submitting these emotions to Holy Spirit for His counsel?

What is the root of these emotions?

What has been the outcome of experiencing these emotions outside the will of God?

How do I cope when these emotions come up?

Idolatry of Emotions Part ll: The Strongman

"The strong man is one who controls a stronghold—a place or territory under his influence." Archbishop Nicholas Duncan-Williams

In Matthew 12 starting at verse 22, we see a story of a man who is demon possessed. The Pharisees accuse Jesus of only casting out demons with power from satan. This is when Jesus begins to explain how a Kingdom divided against itself cannot stand. Essentially, if he was a worker of satan, why would he be casting out satan. Clearly, around Jesus, the Pharisees should have learned to not only think before they speak but think before they think. Jesus goes on to provide strategic insight on how He cast out demons by the Spirit of God. "Or else how can one enter into a strong man's house, and spoil his goods, except he first binds the strong man? And then he will spoil his house" *Matthew 12:29 (KJV)*. This passage, and specifically, this scripture reveals a lot of insight concerning a strongman.

Oftentimes when things occur in our life we tend to pray against or bind the manifestation of the thing and not the root. For example, anyone that has fallen into watching pornography might pray and come against pornography and masturbation, when the occultic strongman working for satan is really perversion by way of the spirit of lust. Pornography is just a tentacle, and cutting off that tentacle won't stop another tentacle from growing in its place to torment and ultimately kill, steal, and destroy.

"But if I cast out demons with the finger of God, surely the kingdom of God has come upon you. When a strong man, fully armed, guards his own palace, his goods are in peace. But when a stronger than he comes upon him and overcomes him, he takes from him all his armor in which he trusted, and divides his spoils. He who is not with Me is against Me, and he who does not gather with Me scatters. "When an unclean spirit goes out of a man, he goes through dry places, seeking rest; and finding none, he says, 'I will return to my house from which I came.' And when he comes, he finds it swept and put in order. Then he goes and takes with him seven other spirits more wicked than himself, and they enter and dwell there; and the last state of that man is worse than the first."" Luke 11:20-26 (NKJV)

As you've read, you can synthesize that the strongman is a high-level demonic spirit that oppresses people and the stronghold is what he controls. The strongman is the ruling spirit and there are several subservient spirits that work for and report to the strongman. An example of a strongman is any gang, or mafia plots we see in movies and that happen in real life: The guy at the top calling all the shots is always hidden or protected in some way, as whatever three letter agency seeks to take down the organization. They take out the little guys one by one, with every confession working their way up to the covert leader. Finally, one day the leader makes a mistake and gets caught, thus shutting down the whole operation. This is how a strongman functions.

When I consider the deep idolatry of emotions I have personally experienced and witnessed throughout my bloodline, I cannot help but see my obedience to emotions as the strongman in life. Yes, although my dysregulated emotions are not what the Bible considers a strongman, what I discovered was that to find success in the areas of emotional regulation, I treated this process like I would any other spiritual strongman controlling a territory. At this point I would ask *you* to think of a ruling spirit or obstacle that seems to control your life, or that you can identify as the source of all your problems. While you think about that, let's examine my life as an example; the sacrificial example, if you will:

The idols in my life move and operate in tandem. I noticed that when I became emotionally dysregulated, I tended to impulse shop after or before I ate what best made me happy, then I would block God out by watching or listening to whatever satisfied my flesh, followed by lust joining the carnal party as I satisfied myself or found someone to do it. To end with a sleep that would ensure I didn't have to confront a Holy Spirit conviction while in my drunken state of emotions. This has been the pattern of my life since I was a teenager. The thing about identifying patterns is just that. You've *just* identified them. The real courage is what you decide to do about the patterns that have been detected. It wasn't until about a year after I detected these patterns that I found the courage to combat them. Proverbs 6:31 tells us that when a thief is caught, he must restore sevenfold and give up everything in his house. I caught the thief, but I didn't know what was next. I knew a sevenfold restoration of everything this somewhat "strongman" (my dysregulated emotions) took from me was due, but I didn't know how to collect what was due. Oftentimes people read this scripture and think this is automatic. Just like the children of Israel in 2 Chronicles 20, even though the battle was fought and had been won, I still had to first show up for victory and collect my spoil. Here I am, in this chapter to not only collect the rest of my spoil, but to also teach you how to collect yours.

I alluded to it above, in every stronghold, there is a ruling or chief spirit, my strongman was my emotions, and it impacted every area in my life. They weren't bad or negative emotions; they were God given and appropriate for my life experiences. The problem was the way in which my emotions were perverted in efforts to drive me to place them above God. For example, food is not bad, we need it to survive. Sleep is not bad; we need *it* to survive. Music is not bad, God created it. The strongman took these inherently *good* necessities and perverted them. (Perversion simply means to be altered from a different state) Disclaimer: Emotions are a part of the soul: mind, will, emotions. Because the enemy is after our soul; our mind, will, and emotions are great targets in his desire to destroy us. The enemy attempted to corrupt Jesus when He was most vulnerable, the devil targets us when our emotions are at its highest or lowest, never when they're stable. This strongman in my life had legal rights through a territorial covenant that was a bloodline iniquity spanning multiple generations. Everyone I knew was a slave to their emotions. A true perversion of how God intended emotions to be used. Perverse emotions were my strongman and its goons controlling my life–all my proclivities, some started and perpetuated by me and some in my bloodline.

"The enemy pairs our emotional distress with our vices." Ezekiel Azonwu

We are so full of patterns, we simply don't pay attention to them. If we stopped to examine our lives and ask questions, I believe we would see the things Holy Spirit is usually quenched from saying. With that in mind, once I stopped to examine these patterns I realized I could find success. After I discovered the monotony in the patterns, God gave me Holy Ghost strategy while showing me Matthew 12:29 in real time and it wouldn't be until later that I would discover the verse to explain my actions. *"Or else how can one enter into a strong man's house, and spoil his goods, except he first bind the strong man? and then he will spoil his house." Matthew 12:29 (KJV).* Through the consistency of the patterns the thief or the strongman was caught, but in order to collect, I was going to need to bind him up (Matthew 16:19). That's when I got a strong revelation through a ministry I follow, Covered by God with

Prophetess Tiphani Montgomery. She created a YouTube video called, *What to Do When All Hell Breaks Loose.* The revelation she shared came from Jeremiah 23:29. It reads, *"Is not My word like a fire?" says the LORD, "And like a hammer that breaks the rock in pieces?"* She was explaining the significance of praying prayers repeatedly using the word of God when you are trying to kill a stronghold. She mentioned that this prayer should be prayed like we are told to take antibiotics–three times a day until the "rock" or "stronghold" was broken into pieces. I wrote down a prayer and decided to strike that rock of unsubmitted emotions in my life.

Strike The Ground

"Then he said, "Take the arrows"; so he took them. And he said to the king of Israel, "Strike the ground"; so he struck three times, and stopped. And the man of God was angry with him, and said, "You should have struck five or six times; then you would have struck Syria till you had destroyed it! But now you will strike Syria only three times."" II Kings 13:18-19 (NKJV)

Strategic Prayer (Pray this 3x a day for 7 days):

God, you said your word is like fire, like a hammer that breaks the rock into pieces. So, Father, I come to you today to insist your word break the stronghold of unsubmitted emotions in my life. But before I pray into my request, I want to first say thank you. My words will never be enough so I vow to worship you in my lifestyle and the way I lift your name so you can draw all men to you. Father, I then ask for forgiveness, forgive me of my sins, iniquities, and transgressions. Father, you said I could ask for forgiveness on behalf of my forefathers, and you would remember us, so concerning both bloodlines running through me, I ask for forgiveness on behalf of my forefathers and as them. Father forgive me of pride, I don't want you to ever oppose me, so kill it off me instead, in Jesus' name. Replace it with humility, help me to go lower in you according to 1 Peter 5:6. Father, also make me unoffendable and impenetrable to the enemy and his schemes. Lastly, Father forgive me for murmuring, complaining and unbelief. I am a lowly servant that needs your forgiveness and full deliverance in these areas.

Now God, with the authority of Jesus Christ I speak to the stronghold and strongman of unsubmitted emotions in my life and according to scripture, I speak the word of God, comparable to a hammer and fire. I declare you to dismantle, disassemble, and destroy this stronghold now. I thank you God that as I strike the Shepherd, the sheep's or idols attached to this strongman will scatter including, but not limited to: lust, impulsive shopping, needing validation, rejection, obsession with marriage or relationship, sleep, entertainment as a pacifier which is social media, tv, and music, and over-indulgence or gluttony of food. But they won't scatter and form greater idols, they will scatter and run back to the pits of hell to be sealed there permanently with the blood of Jesus. Because they are sealed there, I decree that 1000 generations after me will never have to experience this strongman or these idols that are attached to these strongholds.

Now according to Hebrews 11, I will frame the world I want to see. Emotions, hear the word of the Lord, you will align to the will of God. You will submit and subject yourself to God. You will not go rogue. I call you into forever alignment with God's plan for my life and I command you to live there permanently. I call my emotions new. You will never return to Egypt. God is your regulator now. I am not double-minded. I have the renewed mind of Christ. God, I ask you to replace this emotional idolatry with your perfect will for my life. God, to answer your question, these dry bones will live. I prophesy to the dry bones of Godly regulated emotions... "I will put muscles and tendons on you and bring flesh upon you, cover you with skin and put breath in you; and you shall live. Thus says the Lord God: "Come from the four winds, O breathe, and breathe on these slain, that they may live" (Ezekiel 37 (KJV)). Thank you, God, for opening the graves of these dry bones and causing the Godly regulated emotions to come up from their graves, and into the land of Israel [Kayla].

Thank you God that now these dry bones will live, through faith, I now understand that the prison that my emotionally healthy marriage was kept in, that my finances have been kept in, that my health has been kept in, that opportunities I was too emotionally immature to handle have been kept in, that unregulated emotions has been kept in will be forced to release me and my bloodline now!

The thief has been caught, and I command he pay sevenfold and all that's in his house. Father, judge this matter quickly and avenge me and my bloodline speedily. Restore to us everything that was stolen according to Isaiah 54 and Joel 2:18-27.

Cover me now and forever with the full armor of God and with the blood of Jesus Christ as your word has now broken the rock/stronghold and idols into pieces and destroyed the strongman. Thank you, God, that I will see this prayer work and in action immediately. I come against any backlash, retaliation or sabotage concerning this defeat of the enemy. May my children to 1000 generations in our Goshen of healthy and Godly regulated emotions be able to thank God for the work you had your servant [Kayla] do. May all the adults and children I meet be able to regulate their emotions for life because of my example. In Jesus name, amen.

**Now praise the Lord in advance for the victory from the warfare prayer that you have just prayed.*

Tips As You Structure Your Own Prayer:

**It doesn't have to be this long. God is not after the length of your prayer; He is wanting your fervent and consistent prayers.*

Whether your prayer is one sentence or one page. Pray it three times a day for seven days and watch God move!

1. Start with thanksgiving: Even in the presence of an Earthly king, supervisor, mentor, etc., you would thank them for their time, who they are, the opportunity to commune with them so why not approach God the same way?

"Enter with the password: "Thank you!" Make yourselves at home, talking praise. Thank him. Worship him."

Psalms 100:4 (MSG)

"Enter into His gates with thanksgiving, And into His courts with praise. Be thankful to Him, and bless His name." Psalms 100:4 (NKJV)

2. Repentance: I personally like to repent to God before I make my request known (this step can also be found within the Lord's prayer in Matthew 6). In addition, as you repent, agree with your adversary quickly, whatever you're being accused of in the courts of Heaven, agree with the adversary so you can move on to your acquittal.

"From that time Jesus began to preach, and to say, Repent: for the kingdom of heaven is at hand." Matthew 4:17 (KJV)

"If we confess our sins, he is faithful and just to forgive us our sins and to cleanse us from all unrighteousness." 1 John 1:9 (NIV)

"The Lord is not slow to fulfill his promise as some count slowness, but is patient toward you, not wishing that any should perish, but that all should reach repentance." 2 Peter 3:9 (NIV)

"I, even I, am He who blots out your transgressions for My own sake; And I will not remember your sins. Put Me in remembrance; Let us contend together; State your case, that you may be acquitted." Isaiah 43:25-26 (NKJV)

"Agree with your adversary quickly, while you are on the way with him, lest your adversary deliver you to the judge, the judge hand you over to the officer, and you be thrown into prison." Matthew 5:25 (NKJV)

3. Repent on behalf of your bloodline: What is all this for if we are the only ones in our families to experience freedom. Leviticus 26:40-42 said we can repent on behalf of our forefathers and God would be faithful to *remember* us. What a beautiful thing to be placed in God's memory because of your repentance on behalf of your bloodline.

"But if they confess their iniquity and the iniquity of their fathers, with their unfaithfulness in which they were unfaithful to Me, and that they also have walked contrary to Me, and that I also have walked contrary to them and have brought them into the land of their enemies; if their uncircumcised hearts are humbled, and they accept their guilt—then I will remember My covenant with Jacob, and My covenant with Isaac and My covenant with Abraham I will remember; I will remember the land." Leviticus 26:40-42 (NKJV)

4. Kill Pride as Often as You Remember: Our flesh is naturally prideful. We must always go through great lengths to kill pride, asking God to search your heart daily (Psalms 139:23-24).

"If My people who are called by My name will humble themselves, and pray and seek My face, and turn from their wicked ways, then I will hear from heaven, and will forgive their sin and heal their land." 2 Chronicles 7:14 (NKJV)

"But He gives more grace. Therefore He says: "God resists the proud, But gives grace to the humble." James 4:6 (NKJV)

5. "God make me unoffendable": This is one of my daily prayers as offense easily builds a wall of unforgiveness, bitter-

ness, and resentment. On the other hand, causing someone to be offended –well Jesus is clear concerning what this person ought to do.

"A brother offended is harder to win than a strong city, And contentions are like the bars of a castle." Proverbs 18:19 (NKJV)

"Then He said to the disciples, "It is impossible that no offenses should come, but woe to him through whom they do come! It would be better for him if a millstone were hung around his neck, and he were thrown into the sea, than that he should offend one of these little ones." Luke 17:1-2 (NKJV)

6. Did you know murmuring and complaining is what kept the Children of Israel out of the promised land? What promised land are you being kept from because of your murmuring and complaining.

Additional food for thought: In Philippians 2:14-15 the Bible tells us to do all things without murmuring and disputing so that we may become blameless and harmless. Which means if we are caught murmuring and disputing, we will be to blame and have harm. Some synonyms for blameless are "Without fault, perfect, pure, spotless, beyond criticism, above suspicion." Some synonyms for harmless are safe, nontoxic, benign, nonpoisonous. We can expect the antonym of these words if we are caught murmuring and complaining. In what ways are you experiencing criticism, imperfections in your body, carrying toxins or considered toxic because of your murmuring and complaining?

"Do all things without complaining and disputing, that you may become blameless and harmless, children of God without fault in the midst of a crooked and perverse generation, among whom you shine as lights in the world." Philippians 2:14-15 (NKJV)

7. When it comes to warfare prayers, I like to initially state the spiritual authority in which I come in, because ain't nobody got time for another Sons of Sceva fiasco (See Acts 19:14-20).

"But if the Spirit of Him who raised Jesus from the dead dwells in you, He who raised Christ from the dead will also give life to your mortal bodies through His Spirit who dwells in you." Romans 8:11 (NKJV)

"Then David said to the Philistine, "You come to me with a sword, with a spear, and with a javelin. But I come to you in the name of the Lord of hosts, the God of the armies of Israel, whom you have defied." 1 Samuel 17:45 (NKJV)

8. It's important to speak to the very thing intended to take down in prayer. Repeatedly speak to the thing you're up against in the authority of Jesus Christ. As often as you can, speak those scriptures and declarations as you build up the life you desire.

"For verily I say unto you, That whosoever shall say unto this mountain, Be thou removed, and be thou cast into the sea; and shall not doubt in his heart, but shall believe that those things which he saith shall come to pass; he shall have whatsoever he saith. Therefore I say unto you, What things soever ye desire, when ye pray, believe that ye receive them, and ye shall have them." Mark 11:23-24 (NKJV)

9. Because God reveres His word, above all, his name (Psalms 138:2) it's important to give God's word back to Him. Remind God what He said. This is also necessary for the angels assigned to bring your word to pass. Psalms 103:20 (KJV) says, "Bless the LORD, ye his angels, that excel in strength, that do his commandments, hearkening unto the voice of his word." God's commandments are also His written word. As we pray His word, the angels are hearkening upon the commandments

of the written word we pray. SN: I believe this is what praying amiss can look like (James 4:3). Oftentimes we get so caught up with fancy words, when really, we just need to speak the word of God to see things shift.

"I have set watchmen on your walls, O Jerusalem; They shall never hold their peace day or night. You who make mention of the Lord , do not keep silent, And give Him no rest till He establishes And till He makes Jerusalem a praise in the earth." Isaiah 62:6-7 (NKJV)

10. When taking down an organization, the police, FBI, etc. are always looking for the person in charge—it's the same spiritually. Once the boss is taken down, the sheep will scatter without their chief. Because these are offensive prayers, some forethought to the offensive strategy can be to cancel any new leadership or problems that could potentially sprout up. Pray to ensure the spiritual organization is crippled with no chance of rebirth. Tip: Pray a high level dismantling and destruction to the gatekeepers of the organization first.

"Then Jesus told them, "This very night you will all fall away on account of me, for it is written: " 'I will strike the shepherd, and the sheep of the flock will be scattered." Matthew 26:31 (NIV)

11. What's the point of getting ourselves out of generational strongholds, just to see our grandkids right back into the same footholds and patterns we prayed and fasted the bloodline out of? Praying for and covering the next generation is vital. There are several things my children to 1000 generations will never have to experience because of the prayers I pray now. In fact, I ask that one of my rewards for doing God's work on the Earth are generational blessings in a Goshen for my offspring. An inheritance of prayer, rest, etc. is also what the Bible talks about and can also be handled in prayer.

"Therefore know that the Lord your God, He is God, the faithful God who keeps covenant and mercy for a thousand generations with those who love Him and keep His commandments." Deuteronomy 7:9 (NKJV)

"Then he called for his son Solomon, and charged him to build a house for the Lord God of Israel. And David said to Solomon: "My son, as for me, it was in my mind to build a house to the name of the Lord my God; but the word of the Lord came to me, saying, 'You have shed much blood and have made great wars; you shall not build a house for My name, because you have shed much blood on the earth in My sight. Behold, a son shall be born to you, who shall be a man of rest; and I will give him rest from all his enemies all around. His name shall be Solomon, for I will give peace and quietness to Israel in his days. He shall build a house for My name, and he shall be My son, and I will be his Father; and I will establish the throne of his kingdom over Israel forever." 1 Chronicles 22:6-10 (NKJV)

"A good man leaves an inheritance to his children's children, But the wealth of the sinner is stored up for the righteous." Proverbs 13:22 (NKJV)

12. Now it's time to frame the world you want to see. Find 10-20+ scriptures that will become the foundation of the world you would like to create. Ex: *"God according to Luke 1:42 you said I could have the fruit of my womb."* and *"God, Psalms 27:13-14 tells me to wait on you and you will give me courage and strength."* and *"Lord, your word in Jeremiah 1:12 says that YOU are watching to see your word to make sure it comes to pass."*

"By faith we understand that the worlds were framed by the word of God, so that the things which are seen were not made of things which are visible." Hebrews 11:3 (NKJV)

13. It's also important to create parameters, give direction to your blessing and to the devil ensuring he understands his boundaries for your blessing (take your authority and tell the devil where he can go (TO HELL!!)). *"Satan, this far you may come and no farther!"*

When God does the very thing, you have been praying for, the enemy is always close with double-mindedness to make you second guess the blessing from the Lord. Call your mind from double-mindedness and declare you have the sound and renewed mind of Christ.

"When I fixed My limit for it, And set bars and doors; When I said, 'This far you may come, but no farther, And here your proud waves must stop!" Job 38:10-11 (NKJV)

"But let him ask in faith, nothing wavering. For he that wavereth is like a wave of the sea driven with the wind and tossed. For let not that man think that he shall receive any thing of the Lord. A double minded man is unstable in all his ways." James 1:6-8 (KJV)

"Do not conform to the pattern of this world, but be transformed by the renewing of your mind. Then you will be able to test and approve what God's will is—his good, pleasing and perfect will." Romans 12:2 (NIV)

14. Whatever you are currently seeing must be replaced with what you desire to see. When someone is delivered, the unclean spirit that was cast out will always try and return. This is when the maintenance of deliverance must be walked out. The maintenance requires replacing those bad habits that facilitated an atmosphere conducive to activities that would later need deliverance.

'"When an unclean spirit goes out of a man, he goes through dry places, seeking rest, and finds none. Then he says, 'I will return to my house from which I came.' And when he comes, he finds it empty, swept, and put in order. Then he goes and takes with him seven other spirits more wicked than himself, and they enter and dwell there; and the last state of that man is worse than the first. So shall it also be with this wicked generation."' Matthew 12:43-45 (NKJV)

15. Speak to the dry bones of what you're believing in. Ex: "Dry bones of my loveless marriage, I command you to rise up." "Dry bones of my broken family, hear the word of the Lord, I breathe life into you." "Dry bones of my finances, "I put breath in you and you shall live.""

See *Ezekiel 37:3-14*

16. Even if you don't see it, declare that the dry bones are living and declare through faith what is being released through your prayers.

"(As it is written, I have made thee a father of many nations,) before him whom he believed, even God, who quickeneth the dead, and calleth those things which be not as though they were. Romans 4:17 (NKJV)

17. This strongman has stolen too much from you already. Use scripture to legally recover what is yours.

"Yet when he is found, he must restore sevenfold; He may have to give up all the substance of his house." Proverbs 6:31 (NKJV)

E.g.: "I want it all back!" "Give me my stuff back."

18. While this whole prayer has been taking place in the courts of Heaven (as an intercessor, you are a lawyer in the courtroom) ask God, the judge of all judges to judge this matter speedily and avenge you quickly.

"Then He spoke a parable to them, that men always ought to pray and not lose heart, saying: "There was in a certain city a judge who did not fear God nor regard man. Now there was a widow in that city; and she came to him, saying, 'Get justice for me from my adversary.' And he would not for a while; but afterward he said within himself, 'Though I do not fear God nor regard man, yet because this widow troubles me I will avenge her, lest by her continual coming she weary me.'" Then the Lord said, "Hear what the unjust judge said. And shall God not avenge His own elect who cry out day and night to Him, though He bears long with them? I tell you that He will avenge them speedily. Nevertheless, when the Son of Man comes, will He really find faith on the earth?"' Luke 18:1-8 (NKJV)

19. Find scriptures that resonate with the type of restoration and recompense you desire.

"So David inquired of the Lord, saying, "Shall I pursue this troop? Shall I overtake them?" And He answered him, "Pursue, for you shall surely overtake them and without fail recover all."" 1 Samuel 30:8 (NKJV) (See all of 1 Samuel 30)

"God, I want my mind back. I don't want to be anxious and depressed anymore."

"And do not be conformed to this world, but be transformed by the renewing of your mind, that you may prove what is that good and acceptable and perfect will of God." Romans 12:2 (NKJV)

20. Closing the prayer asking God to personally handle any backlash, retaliation, sabotage, etc. because of your prayers. Asking Him to clothe you with the full armor of God. Reminding God, you want to see a quick work and declaring the victory not only for you, but for your children and generations to come. As well as associates and strangers simply because of their proximity to you. Finally, believing your prayers work!

Full Armor of God- See *Ephesians 6:10-20*

"And he believed in the Lord, and He accounted it to him for righteousness." Genesis 15:6 (NKJV)

"But without faith it is impossible to please Him, for he who comes to God must believe that He is, and that He is a rewarder of those who diligently seek Him." Hebrews 11:6 (NKJV)

21. Praise is a weapon!

In 2 Chronicles, chapter 20: God gave them **strategy** to win the war over the enemy. He instructed them to put the praisers before the warriors. As the singing and praises went up, ambushments were sent to the enemy they were scheduled to fight. The same three enemies that conspired against them turned on each other and killed one another; thus, the children of Israel won the war. This proves all we have to do is show up and praise. Through our praise, through our prayer, through our dance, wars are **won**!

In The Spirit of Accountability, Let Me Hold You Accountable?

For seven days straight, set an alarm, make a note whatever you must do to pray this prayer three times a day. Check each time you pray. If this feels like it's doing too much, that's okay, this is what accountability looks like and accountability can be tedious.

Step 1: Identify the strongman in your life and familiarize yourself with his territory (stronghold) in your life. *Please note, this could take some time and require prayer and fasting (Isaiah 58)

Step 2: Identify the sheep or idols surrounding your strongman.

Step 3: Create your prayer.

Step 4: Strike The Rock (Jeremiah 23:29)

Mark each box as you pray 3x daily:

Day 1			
Day 2			
Day 3			
Day 4			
Day 5			
Day 6			
Day 7			

Below I've created some black space for you to reflect on your life, patterns, habits, behaviors, etc. before, during, and after as you witness this move of God manifest in your life through prayer.

Before:

During:

After:

Idolatry of Opinions

"And Elijah came to all the people, and said, "How long will you falter between two opinions? If the Lord is God, follow Him; but if Baal, follow him." But the people answered him not a word." 1 Kings 18:21 (NKJV)

Because an idol is anything we love more than our obedience to God and our worship of something or someone over God; opinions can become idolatry as well. Opinion idolatry is simply obeying the voice of our opinions or other opinions over God's word, which *should* be our first and final authority. In case you weren't aware, God did not ask your opinion when He created the Earth. He didn't ask you if the sky should have been yellow instead of blue. He didn't ask you when He decided to give us two eyes and one nose. If I can be frank, He probably doesn't care what you think concerning your kingdom assignment. He has created you, therefore He knows the gifts and talents He's placed on the inside of you and just like the potter He is, it is His prerogative to mold you into what you ought to be for your assignment.

I heard it said like this, "It wasn't a press conference, nor a board meeting when God called you." When God said, "Let *us* make man in our image, rest assured, you were not a part of the "us"" (Genesis 1:26). He didn't ask your opinion before He formed you as a prophet to the nations; just like He didn't ask Jeremiah when He called him. He didn't consider your feelings when He called you to be a teacher of the truth in a world full of false doctrines. Lastly, He didn't ask about your shortcomings or about your family's rank in the kingdom, ask Moses and Gideon. Each time, our opinions rise up contrary to God, danger is eminent. Our barometer of truth gets us in trouble because we don't realize our compass will always be off kilter because we start off as filthy rags (Isaiah 64:6). As mere vapor (James 4:14). It is worth mentioning that He is a God of choice, although I'm sure Job would have chosen *anything* else. It's also worth distinguishing that those who are unsubmitted to the Lord don't count. Their very foundation fails to convict them of these idolatrous truths. Yes, there are instances in the Bible where God considers what mortals have to say, for example when the Children of Israel kept asking for a king, God obliged and gave them King Saul in 1 Samuel 8, and we see how that worked out. When Abraham asked God not to destroy Sodom and Gomorrah, God considered his request, but the Lord couldn't even find ten righteous people in the city. I'm sure there are a few others, but they are few and far in between. For the most part, God is not interested in our opinions. Especially when they supersede or interfere with His plans and desires for our life. I'm not sure about the way the Holy Spirit talks to you, but whenever I have a bright idea that is contrary to God's will for my life, He often tells me, "Kayla, I don't pay you to think." This is my reminder to humble myself before I find myself humbled. This is the perfect segway to share with you all a personal experience I've had with opinion idolatry:

Revelations 12:11

The time, June 2022. The case, Roe v. Wade. The opinion, idolatrous. The news and social media were flooded with people taking sides and letting their stance be known concerning abortion. I knew how I felt about it. I was pro-life, but I respected a woman's right to choose; their right to make their own decision to get an abortion or not. I thought, *while abortions are horrible, I shouldn't judge.* I had a YouTube channel, but I didn't hear the Lord tell me to make a video and speak on it, so I was set on keeping quiet. At the most, I planned to write a paragraph to post on my social media story, but that was the extent. With all the rhetoric I was seeing, I felt the pro-lifers were too aggressive. I didn't understand why they couldn't understand, "My body, my choice." I felt like I had to say something. So, I took it upon myself to draft a paragraph to post on social media with plans to make a YouTube video later that day. Before I could post my two cents, I got the worst tongue lashing from Holy Spirt I had ever received. It was a Job level fussing out that my little feelings weren't prepared for, the Lord confronted me in the same way He did Job in Job 38:2-3 (NIV) "Who is this that obscures my plans with words without knowledge? Brace yourself like a man; I will question you, and you shall answer me". Suddenly I was the fool Solomon talked about in Proverbs and Ecclesiastes. This is what the Lord said, "How dare you get on a platform I have allowed you to amass influence, subscribers and followers on in *my* name and share an opinion that is contrary to mine. I don't care how you feel about the situation, you speak only when spoken to. If you do decide to speak, it better be aligned to my word. If you want to keep this platform, I suggest you change your "opinions" on abortion. I said it displeases me, so that settles it." I was completely shaken. Who was I to disagree with the one and true living God who has walked the foundations of this Earth, who spoke light and there was light? I now simply ask Him for peace and understanding when I think of the girls and women who are raped and/or become pregnant with their abuser's child. I ask that He provide them comfort and show up as El Roi as He did for Hagar in Genesis 16. I also ask Him to provide other ignorant Christians like me the same revelation He was kind enough to offer me. He could have let me be destroyed by my lack of knowledge and come into agreement with the worship of Molech–a Canaanite god of child sacrifice, but He didn't see fit. In addition to asking God for His grace to be at peace with His sovereignty, I also did some Biblical research on the history of child sacrifice in the Bible. I was able to understand that abortions were more than just, "women's rights," but really the sacrifice to the god of Molech in the Bible. This world tries to justify the murdering of babies, when really it is a new label to ancient sacrificing of children. Back then children were sacrificed for money, fame, success, convenience, advancement and today is no different. I have no interest in convincing anyone of these views, so before I get too passionate, below I have outlined some scripture that can offer additional insight.

A prayer as you read these scriptures, *"Holy Spirit, help me to see this topic through your eyes. Let there be light in my understanding, Amen."*

Jeremiah 32:35, Leviticus 18:21, Leviticus 20, 2 Kings 17:17, Matthew 18:14 to name a few.

Your Opinions Will Hinder Your Purpose

"There will always be a tension between your opinion and God's instructions..." -Michael Todd

The place of your idolatry is sometimes an indication of where God wants to use you to help deliver others. Opinion idolatry tried to stop me from giving birth to ministry, Dancing Wives Prayer Ministry. I was called to and gifted this ministry, but I did not think I was worthy to walk in it. I listened to the lies of the enemy saying, *"You're not married, how can you start a marriage ministry?"* and *"People will laugh at you and not support it?"* These thoughts, in addition to my baseless opinions that consisted of excuses like, *I'll start the ministry after I marry,* almost caused my disobedience to the Lord. The enemy used my past idolatrous footprint of making marriage an idol to almost talk me out of my ministry–the very place where my promise would be birthed. Deep in my deceptive opinions, I couldn't see or remember that I served a God that covered my idolatrous footprints with His righteous and holy footprints. When I stopped faltering between two opinions, it was clear which altar was stronger. In my obedience to God, I started Dancing Wives Prayer Ministry in November of 2023, interceding for marriages, praying with and for wives and wives in waiting all around the world every Sunday at 6pm CST. What I didn't know was that a year later in 2024, I would be getting married in the same month I started the ministry; God rewarded my obedience. I often wonder where my life would be if I continued to make my own opinions a "god" concerning this ministry.

We have many opinions–at our jobs, we get paid for them. In the Kingdom of Heaven, when they supersede or interfere with God's will for your life, they are no good. As you reflect on this chapter, I encourage you to think of the things that you've given your opinion to. Your kingdom assignment, who you sow into, who you vote for, other people's opinion, or even whether or not you are worthy to write a book? It's time to audit your life for opinion idolatry.

1. ____

2. ____

3. ____

4. ____

5. ____

6. ____

7. ____

8. ____

9. ____

10. ____

Prayer:

God, what opinions do I have that are contrary to your will? Search my heart according to Psalms 139:23-24. See if there is any offensive way within me. Where have I made my opinions an idol? Father, whatever you say goes. If it grieves your heart, help it to grieve mine as well. In Jesus' name, amen!

Idolatry in Everyday Life

"Therefore, my beloved, flee from idolatry."
1 Corinthians 10:14 (ESV)

Idolatry shows up in more ways than we realize. It has been so interwoven in our lives and in our society that we don't recognize its monumental footprint. We look at the children of Israel and scoff because we have never bowed down to a golden calf. Failing to realize the addiction to social media is a golden calf, the grief, unforgiveness and bitterness have become idolatry. The spouse and children have become idols in our life. Because we love these things more than God and because God is jealous over us, there will be a showdown. How long will we falter between two masters? We must choose ye this day whom we will serve.

If you're still not convinced that your idols are in fact *your* idols, I will go more in depth about how these idols have affected *me*:

Idol of Food

"Whose end is destruction, whose god is their belly, and whose glory is in their shame—who set their mind on earthly things." Philippians 3:19 (NKJV)

I have always had a nuanced relationship with food. I grew up with a lower middle-class wealth, but a poverty mentality. Even though as the youngest child I only experienced a few years of "The

Struggle," the spirit of struggle stayed with me. By the time my parents had "made it," we were taking family trips to Australia, China, Thailand and Dubai to name a few places. All while still re-using Ziploc bags and paper plates. This poverty mentality made us sit at the table and finish everything on our plate even though we were full, thus normalizing gluttony. As gluttony was normalized, my relationship with food grew more complex. Growing up I was an emotional eater, specifically, a boredom or mindless eater. The summers were the worst for me, because I had nothing to do but eat. My mother and father, bless their hearts, kept me playing sports in all four seasons in an effort to keep weight off me, but I was naturally "big-boned." As I went into middle and high school, the promise of one day seeing my baby fat fall off was an excuse for me to never change how I ate, because I thought, *I'm going to lose it one day soon.* The baby fat never left, and I eventually evolved from a boredom eater to a more profound emotional eater–comfort food was my friend. I never had a problem with eating a lot, just eating unhealthy things and I always ate when I felt an intense emotion, usually sadness. As I moved into college and was introduced to fasting, you can imagine how many stops and starts I experienced when first entering into this new spiritual arena. I realized my stomach was my god, keeping me from my actual God, my Lord and Savior Jesus Christ. I never told my stomach "no"; fasting challenged me to tell my flesh "no." Eventually, by the grace of God, I got better at fasting only to bring me to current life circumstances. In all transparency, currently I'll fast and tell my flesh "no" for a period of time, but when I stop fasting, it's almost as if I'm running back to my long-lost lover because I was being held hostage. Food is the long-lost lover, and God was the one keeping me from my lover. As I am working through this, parameters I have put in place is to pray and or worship after a fast is over. Sometimes I fall short and pop food into my mouth right as the clock strikes, but for the most part I'm thanking God for completing whatever it is I fasted for. This helps me to further exercise dominion over my flesh, establishing who's really in charge. Now, I just have to figure out how to love the food that loves me and hate the food that hates me. Simple enough, right?

As of late, my goal has been to live a fasted lifestyle. To ensure we're on the same page, I will reiterate that a Biblical fast is abstaining from all food for a period of time and only drinking water. A dry fast is abstaining from food and water for a period of time. In the Bible there are so many examples of those that have fasted: Paul's fast in Acts 9:9, Esther's fast in Esther 4:16, and Samuel's fast in 1 Samuel 7:6 to name a few. It's also important to note that there is no such thing as a 21-day Daniel's fast. I'll give you a second to collect your busted bubble off the ground. I did Daniel's fast for years and I had no idea either. In Daniel 1, he lived a consecrated lifestyle of eating healthier foods and he proved this to the king in just 10 days. In Daniel 9:3, we see he *fasted* and set his face toward the Lord to make requests by prayer and supplications, with fasting, sackcloth, and ashes, but the Bible does not say it was for 21 days. On another occasion, he mourned for three weeks by consecrating and denying himself. This lasted 21 days and on day 24, he was visited by an angel (see Daniel 10) and his prayer was answered. Daniel understood that he needed to consecrate and deny himself to seek the Father until something broke and until he got his answer that was being held up. We have combined three separate instances of Daniel's life and made it a worldwide fast. He's probably sitting in Heaven as a part of our clouds of witnesses confused that a generation has mis-interpreted his time of consecration so inaccurately (See the book of Daniel). While any form of abstinence from food or good pleasure is helpful, the Bible clearly states in Matthew 17:21, that this *kind* doesn't go out, but by prayer and fasting. That word "Kind" in the Strong's Greek Concordance translates into "Genos" which means: Kindred, offspring, family, tribe, nation, etc.[3] There are some ancient demons that have tormented bloodlines for generations and we wonder why they have been so successful. It's because the enemy has convinced a generation of people that fasting from television, no fried foods, social media and sex is enough to stop demonic torment. When really, it's the Biblical type of fasting that kills iniquities that have been riding a bloodline for centuries. It's these Biblical types of fasting that quietly and completely banish the strongman over your life. Again, these other consecrations, denials and eating of God's food do wonders in killing the flesh, bringing us closer to God, and centering our lives back on the Lord, but Jesus was clear when He said, "This *kind* don't go out, but by prayer and fasting." Even if you aren't convinced about the translation in the Greek, there's a reason why in verse 17 Jesus addresses the generation when the disciples ask why they can't cure the demon-possessed little boy. *"Then Jesus answered and said, O faithless and perverse generation, how long shall I be with you? How long shall I suffer you? Bring him hither to me." Matthew 17:17 (NKJV).* Jesus understood He was dealing with a generational demon that only respected authority and the killing of flesh through prayer and fasting. As I write this, I am even more convicted; what generational demons have been harassing my bloodline because of my lack of faith to fast? I've digressed, but my intention was to clear any misconceptions to what *fasting* really–as I have no interest in you reading this book and being upset with me for not garnering successful results, such as bloodline deliverance from a multi-generational spirit of depression or narcissism when all you did was give up sweets and social media for 21 days.

To further clarify, this is not a weight issue, this is a heart issue, thus an idol issue. This is a matter of what and whom you wor-

---

[3] G1085 - genos - Strong's Greek Lexicon (KJV). (n.d.). Blue Letter Bible. https://www.blueletterbible.org/lexicon/g1085/kjv/tr/0-1/

ship. This is a spotlight on the thing or person that occupies the seat of your heart. If you're a possible contestant for *My 600 lb. Life* or if you're a beauty queen or wrestler who eats only to binge later. The problem is not the weight; it is the heart. Maturing in the Lord is realizing gluttony comes in all shapes and sizes.

Idolatry of Entertainment

As a therapist, I know my toxic traits very well. In fact, I can identify the root and their functions in my life almost precisely. It's just, I'd rather ignore them. For example: I don't like eating a meal without some sort of noise in the background. I will let my food get cold before I eat it without something entertaining me on one of the multiple screens I own. Why is it that I do this? What is it about the silence that I cannot handle, that I'm afraid to face? Where's my inner peace? What thoughts am I avoiding by not eating in silence? This pattern of questioning opened my eyes to the idol of entertainment I've developed over the years. I've put my desire and need of being entertained above my obedience to God. Deeper than that, whatever is on the other side of the tension of eating in silence is my healing, but I've been avoiding going through it and going around is not an option. God will often request for He and I to share a meal together, but in my carnal mind, I put it in line behind a new episode of whatever is in the top 10 shows. I would prefer to listen to an entire playlist of music or watch an entire series all while promising God to read my Bible after. There is clearly a lowercase "g" god at the seat of my heart. When will I uproot the counterfeit and ask the real God to take His place?

If you were expecting a down by six, half-time locker room speech, I don't have one. It should be abundantly clear that I also struggle with idolatry in some areas of my life. I too am living in the tension of loving two masters. One master will completely overtake my soul and the other will completely make me whole. If you're reading this, pray I choose the master of all masters. Pray, I make a wise and intelligent decision to choose the Lord and to journey to the other side of the tension I'm currently bound by. Pray according to Psalm 34:4 that I seek the Lord and despite my delayed obedience, in His mercy does He answer me and deliver me from all my fears and idolatry.

I Have Two Bridegrooms

Now that I am married, God mirrors our relationship with my earthly relationship. For example, if there is a budding problem in my relationship with God, one pops up in my relationship with my earthly husband. A few months ago, God asked me multiple times to stop watching television to focus more on Him and I ignored Him. One day I heard God saying that it hurt Him that He had to continuously ask me to spend time with Him and that He didn't appreciate having to compete with the idol I had made of television. This confession didn't stop me in my tracks, but sent me further into condemnation, which sent me into rebellion. Not even a few days later, my husband and I got into a huge argument. As I ran to God crying because of this argument where I thought I was completely right, God showed me I was completely wrong. Not only that, He also showed me that the same way I treated my husband is how I treated Him. As tears began to propel down my face, because of the way I hurt my husband, they collided with the "aha" moment from Holy Spirit that was cemented in my mind forever. I was able to see that I had not only hurt my husband, but I also hurt God. I felt even more grieved because I was more upset about hurting a man than I was about hurting God; I had no regard for God's feelings. Thank you, Jesus for Holy Spirit, I then knew, the way back to my husband's heart wasn't just repentance to him, but repentance first to God. I had to take the advice given in Revelation 2:2-6. I had to crawl my way back to my first love. As I spent time repenting to God and falling back in love with Him over the course of a day, my relationship with my husband healed itself. I knew deliverance from idolatry was a daily walk; I just never expected my consequence for idolatry to show up in my marriage. The fear of the Lord is truly the beginning of my wisdom (Proverbs 9:10), especially when it comes to how I show up in my marriage and more importantly how seriously I take my relationship with God. If my relationship with God isn't right, nothing else will be. I still grieve that it took such a drastic parallel for me to understand just how deeply I hurt the Lord, my first best friend, but I'm grateful for His grace.

I said all of that to say, I didn't take the Lord seriously when He told me He felt like He had to compete with television in my life. To me, the television seemed small in comparison to the Lord, but God has created our innermost parts (Psalms 139:13), He knows the very beat of our heart, thus He knows when it beats for another. What I thought wasn't a big deal, was everything to the Lord. An indication if something is an idol for you is if you are having trouble giving it up.

Take an inventory of the things that might be competing for your heart, your time, your devotion:

____

____

____

____

____

____

____

Prayer:

God, what have I put before you? Search my heart according to Psalms 139:23-24. See if there is any offensive way within me. What have I made as an idol that now has the throne of my heart where only you should be seated. Father, if it grieves your heart, help it to grieve mine as well. In Jesus' name, amen!

Idol of Music-B.C.

In the chapter about emotional idolatry, I mentioned that when my emotions are everywhere, I usually have a parade of things I get into as a way of coping with heightened emotions. Listed behind television as number two in my "Little Black Book" of things used to whore after other gods, is music. Music has always seemingly been present to help me cope in any situation since I was old enough to watch the *106 & Park: BET's Top 10 Live.* I would beg my older cousin to burn me a CD of that month's top hits and wear the CD out. I didn't know this was causing a heavy dependence on music, instead of God. When I was sad, music. When I was happy, music. When I was fearful, music. Only when I got older did I realize that God wanted to fill those spaces I reserved for music. Months after this revelation, God would tell me that it felt like I was using music to ignore Him, unfortunately, I was. When spiraling in one of my emotional fits, I would drown my sorrows in old school hits about love or heartbreak. Crying myself to sleep to Marvin Gaye, Teddy Pendergrass, Kem, Luther Vandross, or the Force MDs, I couldn't hear God through the music. I was so drunk with sadness and music was the blanket I cried myself to sleep with. Only to wake the next morning, eyes puffy, but in a sober mind with a new perspective ready to seek God for council. The damage would be done, I had chosen to spend the night with another lover, leaving the lover of my soul, alone. After revelation came a process of conviction. As I continued to spend the nights in my sorrows, drowning in a river of tears & music, I began to get convicted. The ballads didn't console me like they once did. One night I heard the Lord say, "Cry in my arms tonight, please." I turned off the music and cried in God's arms. As my tears hit the pillow it's almost like they watered the garden of perspective and peace. When I cried in God's arms, my crying didn't last as long. It's as if logic zip-locked emotions and I was able to gain perspective that made me want to praise instead of weep. This was Isaiah 26:3 manifested, I kept my mind on God and in return He kept my mind in perfect peace. Philippians 4:7 had a new meaning; it was beyond my understanding that I had peace in situations where my mind should have been gone. Music was losing its seat in my heart, and the rightful God was taking its place.

Idol of Music-A.D.

Before I give an update on my journey with music, I think it's important to add that music is not an inherently bad thing. Music is a powerful tool to usher in the presence of God (See 1 Samuel 16). It's just, I elected music to be *my* god and that was my erroneous doing.

Currently, as my conviction still lingers, (all Glory to God) if I do cry myself to sleep, I leave my spirit open to an impartation from Holy Spirit instead of music. This is not to say I don't have the desire to blast Sam Cooke or Jagged Edge when I'm feeling sad, but I quench this desire before it quenches Holy Spirit. I realize in this idolatry journey I will have to choose my God every time, eventually it gets easier, but a decision always needs to be made. I'm not perfect, so in all transparency on any given day you might hear some 90s and early 00s r&b from my speakers, but this is few and far between. During this time, I have also had to part with songs that aren't conducive to my relationship with the Lord. Have you ever heard a song that didn't glorify God, but it felt good to your soul? That's what music used to be for me. I can tell that access to music has been revoked, it feels good to no longer be a slave to what used to control me; music doesn't have access to a piece of my soul as it once did. I've also come into the realization that music is also a tool the enemy uses to create agreement, alter mood, rehearse lies and more. This makes sense because while God created music, it's likely that Lucifer being an angel with much influence led other angels astray with the very thing God created. In addition, how pridefully on brand would it be for satan, the god of this world (2 Corinthians 4:4) to take something intended to only worship God and use it to glorify him instead? Most of the love songs that we love to love and belt out at an obnoxiously loud volume are idolatrous. Why is it that the writer can't continue to go on without this person? Why are we singing on repeat how our life would be purposeless without a significant other? Why is this song encouraging you to find a love that makes you sick, makes you not want to eat, a love that is a result of bewitchment? A love that only lasts for one night? A stable, healthy love doesn't require such sacrifice. We sing these songs, not understanding we are coming into agreement with idolatry. Am I saying your whole playlist needs to be deleted, that's between you and God. What I will do is challenge you—the next time you are listening to your favorite song, listen carefully to the words. If the song glorifies the god of this world, I'm praying God gives you strength to remove the song from your playlist as well as repent and renounce the lyrics from your life. Furthermore, I'm praying God removes the lyrics from your heart and mind.

If you're not convinced: I once heard a story about a girl who practiced witchcraft. One day she was working on an incantation and as she was scrambling words together to create the perfect spell, she happened to speak the name of Jesus. Immediately, she fell to the ground. Arrested by Holy Spirit, she gave her life to God that night. On her journey with God, like most of us she was saved, but still wanting to be in the world, so she went to the club one night. From being a participant of witchcraft, she knew what the kingdom of darkness looked like, so she was a great agent for God to use in the offense. The young woman said that when a famous rap song came on, she saw the spirits of murder and rage come out of the speaker and jump into the crowd. That night two people were killed. All music carries a spirit. This makes sense because whenever I was sad, certain songs drug me into a deeper pit. Whenever I listened to songs about casual sex, I was ready to give my body to a pretty smile and a smooth talker. Whenever I was listening to music about selling drugs or being a scammer, my 9-5 and small business start-up doesn't seem adequate. Even as a recently married woman, I had to stop listening to songs about creeping and being discontent with your spouse. I realized songs about cheating or calling up an ex should be nowhere near my playlist. I heard it said like this, "Music is the only thing that doesn't need permission to enter into our spirits." -Unknown. God won't let me have a television in my bedroom and even more lately, unless it's to worship Him, He has discouraged me from bringing certain music in my bedroom. Only God knows the portals myself and my family are being protected from by my obedience to Him. It's also worth mentioning that some musical artists (frankly, all spheres of entertainment-actors, producers, directors, etc.) who practice witchcraft openly and privately have attested to offering their songs (work) on the evil altars they worship. They offer their music to their god (the devil) by lacing the beats of their songs with earworms and spells to keep you hooked and bound, in return they are given power, money, fame, influence, relationships, children, etc. The same way satan took Jesus up on the mountain and offered Him the kingdoms of this world is the same way he offers it to us (See Matthew 4:1-11). If this is the case, what ritual or sacrifices are we taking part in by partaking in their music? Ask God to guide you as you reconstruct your playlist.

Idol of Sleep

At this point I can almost see you throwing this book down in frustration because it seems like everything is an idol, to which I would understand. That's how I felt and still feel when I hear God tell me I've made something an idol. Like Paul said, all things are lawful, but not all things are helpful (1 Corinthians 10:23). This is where the idol of sleep becomes a problem. I've always been a sleepy girl, the daycare teacher never had to beg or bribe me to take a nap, I was always the first one down and the last one up. This heightened in college; I began to take naps to avoid stress; my trauma response was to "freeze" and "flop". Literally trying to sleep my life away but waking up to the same problems. I didn't realize that like music, I was allowing sleep to fill a void only meant for God to fill. I used music to ignore God and sleep to avoid Him. God challenged me through Mike Todd's (pastor at Transformation Church) sermon series, *Cuffing Season.* God revealed to me I was "cuffed to comfort." He showed me I was using sleep to avoid the growth that made me uncomfortable. This wasn't something that necessarily started off as a problem, but when I began to make sleep bigger than God, it became a problem. Sleep became the solution and God became an option. It reached a head in a season where I would come home from work every day and sleep three or more hours. I think it's important to add, this was a season I was in idolatry about man and more than likely depressed as well. In retrospect, this was proof the idols in my life had one strongman controlling it all. The strongman didn't care how he got me into the traps of idolatry, it was just important for me to be trapped. In all transparency, I still struggle with this. Every now and then I find myself in this pattern of napping every day. This is when I must reflect on finding the source of my distress. This could take simple reflection, or prayer and fasting, as I ask God to "Let there be light" in my situation. At times, I don't want to pray, "Let there be light." This is when my flesh is battling my spirit and I'm praying rebellion won't have its way. Because sleep is something that is required, this idol is a little more difficult to surrender. Nonetheless, when I keep my love for God on the forefront of my mind–more importantly, when I keep my friendship with God on the forefront of my mind, I have no choice, but to put my flesh on the altar and say no to excessive sleep.

Idol of Anxiety or Sickness

In all transparency, this is an idol I would love to salt-shake out of people. The number of times I hear children of God declare anxiety to be a personality trait is off-putting. Jesus gave us the remedy, yet we decide possession of anxiety is our portion. In Philippians 4:6 *(NKJV)*, God told us to "Be anxious for nothing, but in everything by prayer and supplication, with thanksgiving, let your requests be made known to God." Once we were obedient to that then, "..the peace of God, which surpasses all understanding, would guard your hearts and minds through Christ Jesus." I believe anxiety has been able to become so many people's god because we have not been using prayer and supplication, with thanksgiving, taking our request to the Lord. Therefore, peace has not been able to guard our hearts and minds through Christ Jesus. Jesus is the prince of peace; He cannot dwell amongst anxiety. You cannot have both Jesus and anxiety. Choose ye this day. I don't want to dismiss that some people have experienced some things that rightfully allowed anxiety into the door of their minds, but it should not define you. If anxiety isn't your god, you can take out anxiety and replace it with whatever else this world is telling you to label yourself. As a mental health professional, I appreciate the DSM-5-tr, but I also resent it.

On one hand it provides a name and explanation for real things people are experiencing, and by spiritual law, because these things have a name they must bow to Jesus Christ (Philippians 2:9-11). On the other hand, I live in the tension of not wanting to live in a label as it is not the final authority–it is a report (Isaiah 53:1). As believers, we should use these manuals as a tool, not as our identifier. It is possible to actively treat the symptoms of said disorder or disease, while also actively believing for complete healing. I realize in this world we often put these labels on our kids, our marriages, our lives, not realizing that by virtue of declaring, "I am____" e.g. broke, sick, stupid, etc. in Hebrew it translates to *"hāyâ", which* means "And it came to pass"[4]. If the power of life and death are in the power of our tongue (Proverbs 18:21), why are we speaking death over ourselves and the things and people we love the most? I'm not telling you to be like the saints that ignore the sickness until they find themselves in a hospital. I'm simply encouraging you to not take ownership or come into agreement with what is not yours. Jesus received wounds in his flesh so we could be healed (Isaiah 53:5). Thoughts of Jesus' flesh being ripped off with every weapon those Roman soldiers used should come to mind when you're in need of healing. A Holy Ghost question mark should appear in your mind. *If Jesus was beaten for our healing, why am I not healed?* As you humbly demand your healing on behalf of the finished work of the cross, stay in God's presence long enough to hear the instructions that come with your healing. Jesus was clear with the lepers in Luke 17, so your instructions should be clear as well. These instructions could come with prayer and fasting, a lifestyle dieting change, a doctor's visit to request specific labs, daily praise and worship, or your healing could be miraculous. Whatever your instruction is, God has your answer.

---

[4] H1961 - hāyâ - Strong's Hebrew Lexicon (KJV). (n.d.). Blue Letter Bible. https://www.blueletterbible.org/lexicon/h1961/kjv/wlc/0-1/

Our words and labels have so much power that the Lord told me to stop labeling myself an "empath." If you know anything about Counselors, you know this is difficult because this is the common rhetoric used amongst us to describe our "gifts." God gave me a revelation that because we are encouraged to cast our cares upon Him (1 Peter 5:7) and to exchange the garment of praise for the spirit of heaviness (Isaiah 61:3), calling myself an empath was equivalent to wearing the burdens of people. The Lord revealed to me that under that title, I would have to carry burdens and problems that were never prescribed for me to endure. This is why I felt not only so exhausted trying to love people, but I also felt so tormented by the weight of their problems. I had to come to the realization that not everyone's problem is my problem, even if I do care for them deeply. The same with individuals self-proclaiming themselves apostles, prophets, evangelists, pastors, and teachers. There is a certain level of warfare that comes with those titles. Simply labeling yourself this and walking in an office you have not been called to will bring the warfare and consequences of that label, without the grace or the anointing to walk through it unscathed.

How to Experience a Thing and Not Become It

Jesus experienced anxiety. Luke 22:44 describes Jesus feeling so anxious He began to sweat blood. In Jesus' anxiousness, He prayed more. This was even after an angel came to give Him strength. Everything we experience, Jesus already has (Hebrews 4:15), yet and still He sinned not. He didn't let it consume Him, nor did He use it as an excuse to keep Him in bondage. What happened to Jesus in Luke 22 might be an example of what could happen with us. God could take away the thing that makes you more anxious, God could change how you view your situation or He could even take away the anxiety itself. I want to encourage you that even in your praying, if you become exceedingly more anxious and it appears as if anxiety seems to manifest stronger or in other ways, keep praying! Keep doing what Jesus did. Knowing that your prayers are working, knowing that deliverance is coming. I wish I had some fancy three steps secret to experiencing something and not letting it consume you, but I don't. I am confident however, that in prayer God will give you the answers and direction you need to not only be sustained, but to thrive after traumatic and/or simple and complex life experiences.

Language is also important, rather than, "I am ______" or "I have ____".

Try this instead:

"I often/occasionally/sometimes experience ______"

"I've been diagnosed with ______."

"I'm facing ____ in my mind/body."

Even as you change your language, it might be encouraging for you to put a praise on the end of your phrase.

"I often/occasionally/sometimes experience ______, but by His stripes I am healed."

"I've been diagnosed with ______, but God has the final say."

"I'm facing ____ in my mind/body, but with God nothing is impossible."

These are to name a few. My prayer is that you begin to change your language and as you do, you will come out of agreement with the enemy who wants to see you stolen from, killed, and destroyed.

A Prayer:

God, help me to experience things and not become them. Help me to only call myself what you have called me. Show me where I have labeled myself something you have not called me to be and help me to renounce and come out of agreement with it. God show me what to replace these labels I have called myself and found my identity in. I have declared I am anxious for too long. On this day, let Heaven and Earth record, I am no longer anxious (substitute whatever you are experiencing). Show me Father what else I have declared myself and I will separate myself from it as well. I have the mind of God and the peace of God. God, take away everything that is not like you. In Jesus name, amen.

An Idol of Fear

"For God has not given us a spirit of fear, but of power and of love and of a sound mind." 2 Timothy 1:7 (NKJV)

If God didn't give us the spirit of fear, then who gave it to us? No need to answer that, I'll do it for you. It's the devil; the devil offers the spirit of fear because he *houses* the spirit of fear. Naturally, because he wants us to fall, like he did. He tries to push this spirit onto us. A spirit that this world has labeled as "normal" and "okay." A spirit that naturally God detests because it didn't come from Him. Even satan's demons tremble according to James 2:19 at the thought of Jesus because their master trembles as well. The devil is the perfect gas lighter. He'll suggest to you that you're fearful when really it is a projection of how he feels. Here's a reminder that all he can do is suggest, that's why we must take every thought/ suggestion captive. Once you accept that fear, you and him are now in a covenant of fear. Bonded by horror. This is the case because fear not only has a voice, but it has portals connected to it. Fear causes not only sickness, but it attracts negativity and causes the very thing you didn't want to come upon you.

SN: This is why psychics and tarot card readers are so popular and why some *seem* so accurate. They suggest something is in your future and because of the power of agreement and your open door of fear, they have the satanic power to make it happen. This is also why some of them can tell you what your grandma wore on her last birthday because they operate in a familiar spirit that is ancient, it's the same familiar spirit that bullied your grandma and your great-great grandma and led them away from the Lord, but I digress.

In all my rhetoric, I don't want to dismiss the real things we face that come to scare us, but just like I said in the previous section, I want us to choose a sound mind of power and love. Being delivered from idolatry eventually comes down to a choice, we must choose something different. We must choose to grab on to the hem of His garment not knowing what's on the other side.

Those who know me closely know I tend to hold onto fear with both hands at times. Not only was fear passed down through my bloodline, but there are things that have happened in my life that give me the right to be afraid. Recently, the Lord has convicted me. He told me I would need to trust Him despite what I've experienced, seen, and heard. This has been difficult because I was used to letting fear stop me from doing the things God has called me to do. It has run my life for so long I don't know where my reservations end and fear begins. It has been a thief of time, joy, peace, security and so much more. Choking life from the people and things around me; having its way too often. Instead of listening to God when He told me to write a book, I listened to fear tell me that I couldn't and that I would never. Fear told me if I didn't make things happen on my own, they would never happen. The definition of fear in the Strong's Concordance is to be afraid, to stand in awe of, be awed, to reverence, honor, respect. These were the very things that should have been reserved for God, only. Instead, fear had become the thing I stood in awe of. With my new revelation of fear, I often find myself repenting, renouncing, and replacing the spirit of fear. Since God didn't give it to me, I must take away its legal right to speak in and over my life. Looking back, I know God was so displeased with the power I often relinquished to the spirit of fear but thank God for growth. This is an everyday process, while this has been challenging, it has also been freeing. The weight of fear doesn't sit on my chest like the bully it is anymore. With every fear I face, the god of this world and his minions become smaller, and the strength of my God becomes greater. I also know I have been able to conquer the residue of fear off my womb. I am confident my children won't have to endure the same fears that silenced and held me and the generations before me hostage for years. This idol of fear has bowed, and I know it's up to me to ensure it continues to bow before the God in me.

In addition, as I have embarked on this journey of being freed from fear, I've also come to realize that the devil also distorts fear. We live in such a backwards world where we fear everyone and everything else except the great and terrible God (see Nehemiah 1:5 KJV). The God that gives life and takes life away. The God of beauty and the God of destruction. The God that can wipe an enemy out with a finger. This is the great deception of fear. Once this deception lifts, the fear of man will dissolve, and the reverence of God will increase.

Idol of Unforgiveness

"You have no right to remember what God has forgotten."- Apostle Larry Lea

'"For if you forgive men their trespasses, your heavenly Father will also forgive you. But if you do not forgive men their trespasses, neither will your Father forgive your trespasses." Matthew 6:14-15 (NKJV)

Here, I want you to take a moment to reflect and answer these questions. Who have you not forgiven? A parent, a significant other, a sibling, a friend, a teacher, the person who assaulted you, your pastor, yourself, God? Next question, why haven't you forgiven them?

Forgiveness is selfish, but in the best way. This person probably doesn't deserve your forgiveness. They don't deserve to ever talk to you again. They probably deserve to be thrown up under the prison. They probably deserve the whole world to know what they've done to you, but at the beginning of the day, they are still God's child. God asking us to forgive and to forgive is counter cultural. To forgive is bold and brave, unfortunately it's the road less traveled. God takes forgiveness so seriously that He feels if you won't forgive them, He won't forgive you. The level of evil and sin in this world, we cannot afford to be unforgiven by the one with the power to send us to Heaven or Hell. What is God currently and legally unable to forgive you for because you have not forgiven someone(s) else? If you've made it this far in the book, you must trust the Holy Spirit within me. Trust me when I encourage you to forgive them, and to do it quickly. Your unforgiveness is holding you back from the fullness of your relationship with the Father because unforgiveness has become your god. Every day you delay forgiving them, that idol of your unforgiveness grows in strength, with bitterness as its walls and offense as its barbed wire. Daily, you are being fortified by your hatred towards them. No matter how much distance you put between you all, God examines your heart and He finds it displeasing when He detects that you have a spotted and speckled heart of unforgiveness. Also realizing that unforgiveness is meant to turn your heart of flesh into a heart of stone (Ezekiel 36:26-27). When bitterness, resentment, hatred, and unforgiveness are stored in a body, not only will you look sick, but your body can react with the potential to make you physically and/or mentally sick.

I want to share an instance in which I was caught between the tension of not forgiving and forgiving. I want to preface this by explaining that this was a season where God told me I would need to forgive quickly. He mentioned how the enemy, the accuser of the brethren, was waiting in the courts of Heaven to find me in sin, especially unforgiveness. I did my best to forgive immediately and with my whole heart. Additional context is that towards the beginning of this season, God orchestrated that a close friend of mine and her two children stay at my house for a few months. This was a rare sighting because since college, I've gotten roommate offers and I have always declined them—I like being alone. To break up the comfort of my monotony, it was only right that the Lord himself asked me if I would host this person and her two young children. The add-on bonus from God was that I charge them nothing to stay with me for as long as they needed. I was happy to do it, and I knew the only way we could do it was by the grace of God, especially if we planned to remain friends and even tolerate living with one another. Throughout this time, I knew the Lord was preparing me to live with a husband as well, so I took every lesson with reflection. While we had some great times, it was only right for the challenging times to surface as well. After every offense and before every transgression, I had to recite, "I forgive her, I forgive her, I forgive them" until I felt a release in my spirit. Even in humility I had to constantly ask God for forgiveness as well. Sometimes I would even find myself crying out to God in worship before entering the house, asking Him to give me the words for the conversation I needed to have. Other times I would ask Him to give me words so we could have a healthy confrontation in efforts to keep our friendship, my witness, and honor God at the same time. In this season I had to constantly ask God to remove the bitterness & offense that was building a brick wall of unforgiveness. When the dishes weren't done and we agreed they would be done, I forgave her. When they were loud and I was trying to sleep, I forgave them. When my boundaries were crossed, I forgave them. By the grace of God when my friend and her children moved out, we were able to remain close friends and even laugh about it now. In addition to God showing me how to forgive, He also began to show me that every day in my marriage, I would need to forgive my husband and even myself for our fleshly part of the covenant and He was kind enough to allow me practice with my house visitors. Now, I recite forgiveness in traffic, at work, with family and more. I am constantly declaring by faith, "I forgive ____, I forgive ____, I forgive ____." It often doesn't feel like I have forgiven because the anger or disappointment might still be present. Sometimes I even have to ask God to help my heart feel what my lips are declaring, but I do this so Heaven and Earth can record that I am releasing this person into the freedom of my forgiveness. My forgiveness as a match, burning the court documents the accuser of the brethren is presenting in court with just cause for my eternal damnation. God is the best teacher because just as I did on the practice test, now, as a married woman, I see how the bricks of offense cause walls of unforgiveness. I see how easily resentment builds. Often reciting, "I forgive my husband, I forgive my husband, I forgive my husband."

SN: In that season, outside of my relationship with my friend who was staying with me, I found myself repeating this same lesson in multiple areas of my life, with multiple people: God's humility vs. being a doormat. Certain times I stayed quiet thinking "God's going to fight for me, He sees this and He will intervene." Not understanding that God wouldn't do what He gave me the power to do ask Moses in Exodus 14:13-16. Yes, my great defender, Jehovah Gibbor lives, but a loving God would not fight a battle He gave me the tools to fight. In my efforts to "keep the peace," I didn't know God really wanted me to stand up for myself and to advocate for my needs. I thought God would swoop in with a Holy Ghost conviction and the person would fall to their knees in repentance to me and to God begging for forgiveness. When in reality, God wanted me to show them what Jesus the Lion would do. He wanted me to have a Jesus in the temple moment, but I never did. I realized I was being nicer than Jesus in certain situations, when really in the name of

Jesus I was being taken advantage of because I wanted to be "nice." This way of doing things also caused me to develop a revenge seeking complex. Zoe Burnside once said, "People who don't stick up for themselves often want revenge because they failed to advocate themselves in moments passed." In that season, I often found heart growing "secretly" callous as I plotted revenge. Thinking of a way I could passively aggressively hurt them back when really the Bible tells me in Matthew 18:15-20 that I should go to my brother. I failed to understand the fault was entirely mine because I was the one who taught them how to treat me by having foldable boundaries and an "It's okay" response to every offense. People who advocate well for others and themselves are sometimes considered mean, rude, aggressive or direct. Most are offended by their disposition because they themselves wish they could stand up for themselves or even stand firm on their boundaries in such a way. I thank God, He taught me this lesson. No longer will I be a doormat in the "name" of Jesus. With Holy Spirit's help I am sometimes the Lamb and I am sometimes the Lion.

How Does Forgiveness Look?

Let's be practical in all of this, you probably want to know how forgiveness looks. Realistically, it might look and feel as if you haven't forgiven them. It will feel as if you still carry the same hate and resentment in your heart for them, but it's important to understand that forgiveness takes faith. I've heard it said like this, God told His disciples they must forgive seventy times seven (See Matthew 18:20-21) not so we would keep count, but so we could forget the count. By faith you are releasing them into the freedom of your forgiveness. In your act of faith, God will honor your words, more importantly your heart. Your slate in the courts of Heaven will be immediately wiped clean and one day you will wake up and the burden of unforgiveness will be removed.

For those of you that believe you don't need to forgive anyone else. You, like me, feel that you hold no ought against any man. I want to caution you to examine your heart daily, more importantly ask God to search your heart daily (Psalms 139:23-24). As He does this, Holy Spirit will bring to your mind whom you have yet to forgive. Even if it's a pinch of unforgiveness, remember it's the small foxes that spoil the vine (Song of Solomon 2:15). When He brings these people or this person to mind, take the steps to forgive them, even if that person is you. I completed a "Forgiveness Fast" with Prophetess Tiphani Montgomery's ministry, *Covered by God* in August 2024. I felt I had no one else to forgive, but God asked me to do it anyway. During this time there was one person that I had completely blocked out of my mind from a past relationship. God instructed me to recite their name as I prayed for the faith to forgive them. During the three days I fasted to forgive them, I saw this person every day for three days. I had gone months without seeing them, but while I was fasting, they showed up at the same places I happened to be for THREE. DAYS. STRAIGHT. That's how I knew this fast was working and that they were being used by the enemy to pick on me. When this person showed up to these three various events, it's almost like they were taunting me. They were trying to get to me through my friends, social media, etc. during these three days. During one of my weeping sessions to God, I told Him it felt like He was letting the devil sift me. God assured me that He saw what the enemy was doing. He said that it was a Leviathan and Jezebel spirit mixed (Narcissism) and it had set its sights on me. He instructed me to finish the fast in a strong manner and God asked if I would let Him be my vindicator instead of handling it myself (in transparency I was ready to cuss them out if they showed up on the fourth day, don't judge me). The ministry I was fasting with had a motto for that fast, "Play Dead." The Prophetess explained that the enemy couldn't kill a dead man. So, I killed my flesh and took the sifting knowing that in Luke 22:31, Jesus said He was praying that my faith would not fail and when I got through the time of testing, I could strengthen those behind me. During these three days, the option to hate this person more felt tempting, but instead, God gave me the grace to forgive them more aggressively. It was only grace that carried me through this fast because it was on the first or second day, I found myself ready to give up. In my emotional tornado, I found myself at my favorite restaurant ready to throw in the towel and eat. I got a text from a friend doing it with me encouraging me not to give up. Before the lady finished heating up my tortilla I ran out of the restaurant. On day four it was like the sifting had lifted. I saw the person again and I felt not only peace, but I felt so sorry for them. My intercession for them increased because I was able to see how tortured by the enemy, they really were to do what they did to me. Three weeks after this fast, my husband direct-messaged me on social media. Three months after that, we got married! What would have been my lot if I chose to stay in that unforgiveness?

Begin Your Journey to Forgiveness:

1. Ask God for forgiveness.

2. Forgive yourself.

3. List all the people you need to forgive.

4. Anyone on that list that causes you to have a visceral reaction when you think of them, start with them first.

5. You will more than likely need to pray and fast. (Ask God to remove the layers of protection you've surrounded yourself in to avoid thinking about them. Ask God to expose the parts of you not pleasing to Him).

6. Spend time in prayer asking God to help you forgive them. Take the memory of what they did out of your body, soul and spirit.

7. Find yourself in repentance to God daily according to Psalm 139:23-24.

8. Repeat as necessary.

After these steps are complete, write a "By Faith" statement:

By faith, I forgave ____________. With the authority of the blood of Jesus, I declare that the memory of their betrayal is removed from all systems in my body that house memory. They are now released into the freedom of my forgiveness forever, amen.

(Add whatever else to this prayer that is necessary for your forgiveness)

Idol of Offense

By definition, an offense means, "Annoyance or resentment brought about by a perceived insult to or disregard for oneself or one's standards or principles." I want you to think of a person or thing that annoys you. Next, I want you to think of a situation or person you resent. There lies your offense. While there are some offenses that reveal the evil spirits in operation within our hearts. There are other offenses that naturally come from the Gospel of Jesus Christ, meant to offend us for the purpose of evolution and growth. Just as Jesus' very name being mentioned offended the Pharisees, Sadducees and anyone else who chose not to believe in the evidence of God working through Jesus Christ. In Matthew 13:41 by Greek definition of the word, "Offend" translates to *"skandalon"*. This word also applies to Jesus Christ, whose person and ministry was so offensive and contrary to the expectations of the Jews concerning the Messiah. It was so offensive that they rejected Him and by their obstinacy they made shipwreck of their salvation. No wonder when you walk in a room in the authority of the same spirit that raised Jesus from the dead, many are offended by your confidence. No wonder when someone makes a comment that is meant to expose the evil spirits in you, you rise up with a spirit of offense and cannot contain your anger. The body of Christ is unfortunately full of offense. Most seem to be offenders or builders of offense, sometimes both. Offense is a sneaky demon that camouflages itself in efforts to never be cast out. Today is the day of eviction. Let Heaven and Earth record, *"OFFENSE, NO MORE HIDING! WE SEE YOUR UGLY HEAD AND WE CUT IT OFF: IN OUR CHURCHES, IN OUR RELATIONSHIPS, IN OUR HEARTS. WE BIND YOU AND ALL THAT'S ATTACHED TO YOU AND LOOSE YOU BACK TO THE PITS OF HELL WHERE YOU BELONG. God, I ask you to replace offense with joy, kindness, and humility. God, search me daily for offense that grows like wildflowers in the field of my heart. I don't want to be offended and if I offend, please help me to right my wrong, in Jesus' name, amen."*

See Luke 17, Proverbs 18:19

Idol of Grief

Only those who mourn truly are able to move on and experience life again. -Unknown

"And I set my heart to know wisdom and to know madness and folly. I perceived that this also is grasping for the wind. For in much wisdom is much grief, And he who increases knowledge increases sorrow." Ecclesiastes 1:17-18 (NKJV)

The idol of grief is one of the more widely acceptable idols. Grief is digestible because death is a part of life. Because grief is so common and understandable, it often overstays its welcome and causes our heart to stray from the one who promised to be close to the broken-hearted (Psalms 34:18). Grief is not linear, but very much cyclical. One day you could feel acceptance and the next, anger. The problem is not grief; Jesus grieved; the Garden of Gethsemane is proof. The issue arises when grief becomes a god of our heart. When grief overcomes us to the point where it becomes a character trait or a sense of our personality. When we are associated or widely known by our circumstance and not by our God, there is the error. Society has made prolonged grief a common disorder, but this goes against what God would have for us. Jesus shows us how we are to grieve a person in John 14. We are to not let our hearts be troubled, but we are to know that Holy Spirit will be with us in their absence as He has always been since Jesus' death. 2 Corinthians 5:8 also tells us that to be absent from the body is to be present with the Lord. By faith we can only hope that the person we are grieving is with the Lord.

If I can be honest, I am not yet qualified to talk about grief as I haven't had much loss in my life. I use the operative word yet, because I know it is a part of life. As a student to Holy Spirit's teachings, I have found a common principle concerning grief. I'll share this principle through the eyes of being an onlooker to someone else's pain:

My Apostle's husband passed away a little less than a year before I joined their church. Where most women would waste away with grief, in the strength of the Lord she picked up a grieving church as well as her own family and soldiered on. When I learned of her circumstances in the first few months of joining the church I couldn't help but think about the norm in other countries: They encourage women to begin wearing black, isolate themselves from society, and it's widely known that life stops when the husband dies. I soon came to realize this practice in various societies to be an idol of grief. Every Sunday my Apostle would get on stage under the influence of Holy Spirit, in the midst of worship, with her eyes heavy from laying in the presence of the Lord and instead of questioning why her husband had to die, she would stand there and bask in the goodness of God. She would openly declare, "I don't worship God because of my circumstances, but I worship God because of who He *is*. If I praised God because of my circumstances, I wouldn't have been able to get out of bed this morning, but I owe Him a sacrifice of praise." She would go on to say, "I'm still standing because my hope is in God, if I put my hope in a man I would've wanted to die with my husband. But my hope was never in him, my hope was always in the Lord, that's why I can praise and worship Him in spite of." At this time in my life towards the end of 2022, her open declaration was revelatory to me because I didn't know the importance of putting my hope in God, rather than a man. All my life, I was taught by society to put my hope in man. The idol of grief wanted to squish her with its thumb, but in her worship, she said no. By saying no, and living her life out loud, she cleared some of the idolatrous haze I was living under. In the spiritual realm, she was waging war on *my* idols. I thank God that He gets His glory out of any circumstance and any situation, all we must do is step out of His way. Through her testimony, I overcame him [satan] by the blood of the lamb and by the sharing of the testimony. In her victory over grief, she showed me and all who paid attention that it was possible to focus on the Lord and not the death of our loved one. I was taught that even in the pangs of death, God was due a praise and a sacrificial worship. I learned how to command my soul to praise the Lord when my flesh said, "not today.".

Something worth mentioning when it comes to grief is that it doesn't just revolve around the loss of people. Grief can also be associated with so many aspects of life we experience. We also grieve situations, relationships, seasons. Grief appears when judgement is questioned, when our past life must be released, when feelings of being lost in life surface, losing traditions and more.

If you're experiencing grief, if you've just lost someone, or something, ensure you are not hyper focusing on the pain, instead focus on the one who is greater than all pains. Don't waste away with grief; instead, offer God a sacrifice of praise and in exchange, he will take the garment of heaviness. Death is a part of life. We all must experience it at one point in time. When you do, remember to wage war on the idol of grief that has swallowed so many whole.

Grief vs. Mourning

Grief and mourning are two terms often used interchangeably, but they are two very different expressions. Grief is the inward experience to loss. It is a deep sorrowful response that is not linear, rather cyclical. Mourning is the outward experience to loss. Mourning is done sometimes collectively. Grief is what you feel, while mourning is what you do.

We Don't Grieve Like the World

"For we believe that Jesus died and rose again, and so we believe that God will bring with Jesus those who have fallen asleep in him." 1 Thessalonians 4:14 (NIV)

In 1969, Elisabeth Kübler-Ross wrote a book called "On Death and Dying." Within that book, she outlined these 5 stages of grief: denial, anger, bargaining, depression, and acceptance. In 2019, David Kessler who co-authored the book with Kübler-Ross expanded the model in his own book entitled "Finding Meaning: The Sixth Stage of Grief. In this book he added an additional stage, "meaning." Since we don't grieve like the world, I think it could be important to have tools as you experience the 5 stages of grief + 1 more and not get stuck in its cycle. With the help of Holy Spirit, I'm going to outline these 6 stages of grief in a way we as believers can experience them with fidelity yet still hold our allegiance to Christ.

Denial:

Denial in grief typically looks like someone who is emotionally numb and not able to process what has happened. This could be a person shutting down, avoiding any reminders of the loss and distraction to evade reality. While in the Kingdom, God doesn't expect you to ignore this step, rather invite Him into your process. Denial in the Kingdom looks like acknowledgement. Instead of suppressing the feelings of loss, God encourages us to take our pain to him and even explain our discomfort and/or confusion.

Practically:

This looks like honestly confronting the Lord like the Shunamite woman in 2 Kings 4, like Jesus in Matthew 27:46, and like David in some of his poetry in Psalms, specifically Psalms 22. This can be done in a personal journal where you can freely write out all you feel, holding nothing back from a big God or spoken out loud to God in your secret place.

Scripture:

"But when she reached the Holy Man at the mountain, she threw herself at his feet and held tightly to him. Gehazi came up to pull her away, but the Holy Man said, "Leave her alone—can't you see that she's in distress? But God hasn't let me in on why; I'm completely in the dark." Then she spoke up: "Did I ask for a son, master? Didn't I tell you, 'Don't tease me with false hopes'?" He ordered Gehazi, "Don't lose a minute—grab my staff and run as fast as you can. If you meet anyone, don't even take time to greet him, and if anyone greets you, don't even answer. Lay my staff across the boy's face."" 2 Kings 4:27-29 (MSG)

'And about the ninth hour Jesus cried out with a loud voice, saying, "Eli, Eli, lama sabachthani?" that is, "My God, My God, why have You forsaken Me?"' Matthew 27:46 (NKJV)

"How long, O Lord? Will You forget me forever? How long will You hide Your face from me? How long shall I take counsel in my soul, Having sorrow in my heart daily? How long will my ene-

my be exalted over me? Consider and hear me, O Lord my God; Enlighten my eyes, Lest I sleep the sleep of death;" Psalms 13:1-3 (NKJV)

Anger:

Anger is a natural emotion that is common in grief. Often anger is found in oneself, with God, with other people, and often, with that person that has died. A way to rewrite the patterns of anger in grief is to lament. To lament simply means to passionately express grief or sorrow. To lament like those in the Bible can be done in four simple steps: address God, state your complaint, make your request known, express your trust of God no matter the outcome. Following these steps allows for a believer to be angry, yet not sin. In Psalms 22, David provides a great model for these four steps.

Practically:

Practically, this looks like having an open and raw conversation with the Lord in the height of your anger. What might feel natural is to pin up the anger or to express it through crying or potentially in a harmful way, but what will prove helpful in the long run is to immediately express this to God.

Scripture:

""Be angry, and do not sin": do not let the sun go down on your wrath, nor give place to the devil." Ephesians 4:26-27 (NKJV)

"Be angry, and do not sin. Meditate within your heart on your bed, and be still. Selah" Psalms 4:4 (NKJV)

"Do not hasten in your spirit to be angry, For anger rests in the bosom of fools." Ecclesiastes 7:9 (NKJV)

'My God, My God, why have You forsaken Me? Why are You so far from helping Me, And from the words of My groaning? O My

God, I cry in the daytime, but You do not hear; And in the night season, and am not silent.' Psalms 22:1-2 (NKJV)

Bargaining:

Bargaining often looks at what could have been done differently. It emphasizes a lot of shoulda, coulda, woulda and if, then. Bargaining usually begins with, "If only" and ends with, "God if you... then I'll". In the Kingdom, this could be reframed by trusting, which proceeds surrender. Through faith, bargaining can go from, "God if you would only." to "God, I don't understand this, but I trust you."

Practically:

When a desire to bargain or thoughts of negotiation come about, it's helpful to acknowledge the desired deal and surrender it to God. Ex: "God, I give you these desires and I lay this loss at your feet."

Scripture:

"And she was in bitterness of soul, and prayed to the Lord and wept in anguish. Then she made a vow and said, "O Lord of hosts, if You will indeed look on the affliction of Your maidservant and remember me, and not forget Your maidservant, but will give Your maidservant a male child, then I will give him to the Lord all the days of his life, and no razor shall come upon his head."" I Samuel 1:10-11(NKJV)

"Father, if it is Your will, take this cup away from Me; nevertheless not My will, but Yours, be done." Then an angel appeared to Him from heaven, strengthening Him. And being in agony, He prayed more earnestly. Then His sweat became like great drops of blood falling down to the ground." Luke 22:42-44 (NKJV)

"In those days Hezekiah was sick and near death. And Isaiah the prophet, the son of Amoz, went to him and said to him, "Thus says the Lord: 'Set your house in order, for you shall die, and not live.'" Then he turned his face toward the wall, and prayed to the Lord, saying, "Remember now, O Lord, I pray, how I have walked before You in truth and with a loyal heart, and have done what was good in Your sight." And Hezekiah wept bitterly. And it happened, before Isaiah had gone out into the middle court, that the word of the Lord came to him, saying, "Return and tell Hezekiah the leader of My people, 'Thus says the Lord, the God of David your father: "I have heard your prayer, I have seen your tears; surely I will heal you. On the third day you shall go up to the house of the Lord. And I will add to your days fifteen years. I will deliver you and this city from the hand of the king of Assyria; and I will defend this city for My own sake, and for the sake of My servant David." II Kings 20:1-6 (NKJV)

Depression:

Depression often feels like you're trapped underneath a weighted blanket. It can often feel isolating and usually gives the illusion that it will never end. As a Christian, this can be reframed with a promise of hope from God that He would never leave us nor forsake us, even if we feel forsaken. In a time of depression, may hope in God be the strength that will help you push past the mental weight and torment.

Practically:

Isolation in this stage can be consuming, to counteract this, community is necessary to offer support as you surround yourself with believers that will pray with you, sit with you, laugh with you, and more. Moments of gratitude are also important here, gratitude (and praise) brings joy, joy brings strength–keep a gratitude journal and read it as often as you feel weak, reminding yourself that in your weakness, He is strong (2 Corinthians 12:9-10). Even more practically, whenever you feel the heaviness come upon you, stand up and move your body. Put on a praise song and dance before the Lord or go for a walk.

Scripture:

"Casting all your care upon Him, for He cares for you." I Peter 5:7 (NKJV)

"Come to Me, all you who labor and are heavy laden, and I will give you rest." Matthew 11:28 (NKJV)

"Anxiety in the heart of man causes depression, But a good word makes it glad." Proverbs 12:25 (NKJV)

'Yes, my soul, find rest in God; my hope comes from him." Psalms 62:5 NIV

"You have turned for me my mourning into dancing; You have put off my sackcloth and clothed me with gladness," Psalms 30:11 (NKJV)

"Why are you cast down, O my soul? And why are you disquieted within me? Hope in God; For I shall yet praise Him, The help of my countenance and my God." Psalms 42:11 (NKJV)

"Cast your burden on the Lord, And He shall sustain you; He shall never permit the righteous to be moved." Psalms 55:22 (NKJV)

"Answer me speedily, O Lord; My spirit fails! Do not hide Your face from me, Lest I be like those who go down into the pit." Psalms 143:7 (NKJV)

'"But now, Lord, what do I look for? My hope is in you." Psalms 39:7 (NIV)

Acceptance:

Experiencing the stage of acceptance in the cycle of grief looks like coming to terms with what has happened. While grief is cyclical, this stage seemingly adds an ending to loss. As a Christian this stage should come with an embrace of what you lost and a perspective of eternal life. As a Christian, my hope is that you will be able to rest in the resurrection of Jesus Christ, knowing that while you've lost this person, death is not the end–they have lived to one day live again. In all stages of grief, let hope arise, but especially in this stage, let hope be your guiding light and momentum forward as you learn to live with this loss and live through it.

Practically:

Do something as often as you need to in your loved one's memory, a donation to their charity of choice, artwork, host a celebratory event, etc.

Scripture:

"And He opened their understanding, that they might comprehend the Scriptures." Luke 24:45 (NKJV)

"And we know that all things work together for good to those who love God, to those who are the called according to His purpose." Romans 8:28 (NKJV)

""Go, gather all the Jews who are present in Shushan, and fast for me; neither eat nor drink for three days, night or day. My maids and I will fast likewise. And so I will go to the king, which is against the law; and if I perish, I perish!"" Esther 4:16 (NKJV)

"For I am persuaded that neither death nor life, nor angels nor principalities nor powers, nor things present nor things to come, nor height nor depth, nor any other created thing, shall be able to

separate us from the love of God which is in Christ Jesus our Lord." Romans 8:38-39 (NKJV)

"Not that I speak in regard to need, for I have learned in whatever state I am, to be content: I know how to be abased, and I know how to abound. Everywhere and in all things I have learned both to be full and to be hungry, both to abound and to suffer need. I can do all things through Christ who strengthens me." Philippians 4:11-13 (NKJV)

''He will wipe every tear from their eyes. There will be no more death' or mourning or crying or pain, for the old order of things has passed away." Revelation 21:4 (NIV)

"But he said to her, "You speak as one of the foolish women speaks. Shall we indeed accept good from God, and shall we not accept adversity?" In all this Job did not sin with his lips." Job 2:10 (NKJV)

"I form the light and create darkness, I make peace and create calamity; I, the Lord, do all these things.'" Isaiah 45:7 (NKJV)

"For God so loved the world that he gave his one and only Son, that whoever believes in him shall not perish but have eternal life." John 3:16 (NIV)

Meaning:

Finding meaning might not always equate to receiving answers; there are some things God will only reveal to us in eternity. We can glean from Job that it might not prove advantageous to get so wrapped up in finding answers. A better use of your time might be used rediscovering who God is and all His grandeur.

Practically:

Have you ever been on a first date? Think of the questions you might ask the person sitting opposite of you. That's what you can do with God. Ask God questions as if you were using that information to build a foundation for a relationship. Redefine the meaning of the things you thought you knew.

Scripture:

"And Hezekiah received the letter from the hand of the messengers, and read it; and Hezekiah went up to the house of the Lord, and spread it before the Lord. Then Hezekiah prayed before the Lord, and said: "O Lord God of Israel, the One who dwells between the cherubim, You are God, You alone, of all the kingdoms of the earth. You have made heaven and earth. Incline Your ear, O Lord, and hear; open Your eyes, O Lord, and see; and hear the words of Sennacherib, which he has sent to reproach the living God. and have cast their gods into the fire; for they were not gods, but the work of men's hands—wood and stone. Therefore they destroyed them. Now therefore, O Lord our God, I pray, save us from his hand, that all the kingdoms of the earth may know that You are the Lord God, You alone." Then Isaiah the son of Amoz sent to Hezekiah, saying, "Thus says the Lord God of Israel: 'Because you have prayed to Me against Sennacherib king of Assyria, I have heard.'" II Kings 19:14-16, 18-20 (NKJV)

Idol of Pain

This is a good time to submit to the group chat that we can also make pain an idol. Leah not only found her identity in pain, but she named her children after her pain (Genesis 29). Jabez' mother idolized her pain to the extent of naming her son out of her pain (1 Chronicles 4:9). What pain have you not only founded an identity upon, but is now a paying resident of your heart?

Idol of Shame

Idolatry of shame, like grief is another crafty idol. It is more obvious than grief, but equally crafty. The idol of shame can be described as refusing to walk in the forgiveness that God has bestowed. It's the feeling of desiring more punishment and consequences as if God's measure of consequence wasn't enough. Causing you to live in humiliation and dishonor, when a visitation would have been enough to cause repentance. As God's children, we often repent and even worship buried in our shame. Focusing on how bad we are and not how good He is. Yes, our worship should start with repentance, but it shouldn't stay with repentance. Eventually, we have to lose our focus on what we've done and think about what He's done. Sending His only son to die on a cross, for our shame. The idol of shame is amnesia to scripture that declares we are a new creation; old things have passed away. God is faithful in scripture to even offer us an exchange to shame "Instead of your shame you shall have double honor, and instead of confusion they shall rejoice in their portion. Therefore, in their land they shall possess double; Everlasting joy shall be theirs." *Isaiah 61:7 (NKJV)*. The contingency here is that in order to receive a double portion of honor, it cannot coincide with shame. Shame has caused enough delay in your life. It's time to surrender the shame.

For the next 7 days, 3x a day, I challenge you to surrender the shame. Whether this is a daily declaration in the mirror, naming the shame that has kept you bound or a prayer, asking God to take away the shame and then rejoicing and thanking Him that He has. Use the scriptures below and more that you find as you walk yourself from underneath the cloud of shame:

"For the Scripture says, "Whoever believes on Him will not be put to shame."" Romans 10:11 (NKJV)

""Do not fear, for you will not be ashamed; Neither be disgraced, for you will not be put to shame; For you will forget the shame of your youth, And will not remember the reproach of your widowhood anymore." Isaiah 54:4 (NKJV)

"They looked to Him and were radiant, And their faces were not ashamed." Psalms 34:5 (NKJV)

"In You, O Lord, I put my trust; Let me never be ashamed; Deliver me in Your righteousness. Bow down Your ear to me, Deliver me speedily; Be my rock of refuge, A fortress of defense to save me." Psalms 31:1-2 (NKJV)

""For the Lord God will help Me; Therefore I will not be disgraced; Therefore I have set My face like a flint, And I know that I will not be ashamed. He is near who justifies Me; Who will contend with Me? Let us stand together. Who is My adversary? Let him come near Me." Isaiah 50:7-8 (NKJV)

"Looking unto Jesus, the author and finisher of our faith, who for the joy that was set before Him endured the cross, despising the shame, and has sat down at the right hand of the throne of God." Hebrews 12:2 (NKJV)

I'm so very proud of you. The floor of shame has now become your ceiling of honor. Celebrate yourself for the next 7 days, 3x a day. You have sown in tears; it is time to reap in joy! (Psalms 126:5)

Sororities & Fraternities

If you were met with immediate offense once you saw this subtitle, I challenge you to reflect on these questions before reading this passage or even before skipping this passage:

- Lord, reveal to me all the idols in my heart and in my life.

- Lord, can you please show me any deception in my heart and in my life?

- Why do I get offended when people leave or talk negatively about my sorority or fraternity?

- Did you ask the Holy Spirit if this was an organization you could join? Have you asked Him what He thinks of it now?

- If the Lord is asking you to leave this organization, what is keeping you from obeying?

- What vows or oaths did I take, and what commitments did I make to join this organization?

- Has the pledge/ritual book misused scripture in any way?

I was a member of a Black Greek Organization for 5 years. I didn't know it was an idol because this was something normal in the black community I was raised in. It wasn't until I saw someone post about leaving their fraternity that God began to deal with me about leaving the sorority. I left not because I understood why it was an idol, but I left because my Abba asked me to. I left out of blind obedience before God truly explained the depths of sin I was in. I won't get into the actual Greek gods these organizations represent and bow to, I'll just share on an intimate level, my story:

God told me I could spend my whole life in that sorority, and I wouldn't experience any harm or consequence, but He said my children wouldn't have the same fate. He took me to Exodus 20:5. I thought, *okay, I'll leave when I have children.* This warning from the Lord didn't wane. I begin to get convicted almost every day and my convictions aren't subtle. My convictions make me nauseous, they make me light-headed, and they make me feel like I could go insane if I don't heed the voice of God. God was doing the same with a close friend and former line sister. She felt the convictions too and was prepared to leave, but I wasn't. I told her I couldn't denounce the sorority with her, and this caused friction in our relationship until we both decided to leave, which happened to be about two weeks later. There were so many worldly voices in my head as to why I couldn't leave. I was a legacy. I was extremely involved in the organization on the local and national level. Half of my wardrobe consisted of one or the other color. As I fasted to truly hear from the Lord, He personally told me how much it broke His heart that I had pledged my heart, my mind, and my strength to another. In an instant during worship, I flew through the house putting all paraphernalia into trash bags. I knew if I didn't trash it that night and tell someone for accountability, I would lose my nerve come morning and it would be a cycle. As God would have it, a close friend of mine in another sorority was feeling the same convictions and left her sorority simultaneously. Telling my family, friends, co-workers, and then the world was no small feat. God was tackling the idol of people-pleasing, to part with that idol hurt worse than to leave the sorority. A few months after I left the sorority, God began to bring understanding. I was out one day in the community, and I saw a local chapter of the sorority strolling and I had so much grief in my heart about leaving. God explained my grief to me in a way I could understand. He said, "Kayla, it was like you were married to someone else. You pledged your heart, your mind, and your strength to this man. You served him with every opportunity you had. You wore all *his* clothes and branded yourself with *his* name on your chest. You wore white to your wedding (initiation), you bowed down in a dark room with candles at a physical altar decorated with items to be sacrificed to the founders (gods) and to sign your name to a covenant, calling yourself his. You gave this man your time, talents, and resources. Singing hymns to him as often as he desired. Even going as far as reaffirming your covenant once every 2 years at the national conference. Encouraging others to enter a covenant with him as well, judging those who decided against it. Worse yet, you wear his name in my sanctuary. You applaud leaders in the fivefold ministry who desecrate my pulpits by wearing the name of another god on my altars. Yes, you served the community, but you did it in *his* name with *his* name on your chest. You even offered up your future children to serve him." This broke me down, I felt so grieved to have cheated on God in this way. What else besides repentance can be done when you've wronged God in this way? This is why I choose to cry loud and spare not. So many of Jesus' bride is betrothed to another. Not just the Black Greek Organizations, but multicultural sororities and fraternities as well as free masonry. No matter the name of the god who received your allegiance, or the Greek letters you represent, it has yoked you with the occult and God is not pleased.

I'll leave you with this. God is asking you to choose this day, who you will serve. How long will you falter between two Gods? The altar of the Greek god you bow to, sow into, do community service for, sing about hates *your* God. If God be your God, turn your back on your Greek god and choose life. If your Greek sorority or fraternity be your god, stay with your idol and await your consequences. Soon will come a mass exodus, my prayer for you is that you are in that number of the called-out ones.

Sidenote to the ones that have been called out, you must cry loud and spare not. If anyone has joined a Greek organization because of you, if you do not warn them, the blood is on your hands (See Ezekiel 3:16-27). You cannot leave quietly because you didn't join quietly. However, God is asking you to leave, leave in that way. Partial obedience is disobedience.

A Deliverance Prayer for Friends and Family Who Are Still a Part of Fraternities and Sororities:

Whoever's deliverance you are believing for, put their name in the blank.

God, you said your word was like a fire and like a hammer that breaks the rock (stronghold, idol) into pieces... so, I come to you to ask you to break the idol of sororities and fraternities into pieces, specifically (name one organization or all if applicable). Before I ask for anything, I thank you for knowing my heart and that it's already done. I say thank you in advance, thank you for who you are, thank you for loving me and the people I love and even those who I don't. Father, forgive me of my sins, iniquities and transgressions. According to Leviticus 26:40-42, forgive my forefathers as well. Father put us in remembrance. Lord, today I come to you on behalf of _____. Before I ask for anything, I want to repent on behalf of them, Father forgive them for they know not what they do. God, I want to first thank you that you are rebuking the spirit of validation and of people pleasing from _____. I bind all his/her insecurities and submit them to You, he/she is a very secure man/woman. _____will begin to think more highly of themself and not care what people think. I also want to pray against anything that would keep them attached to the sorority or fraternity even when you have called them out. I pray that when you call them out, they will obey the first time. Give _______ a grace and a strong conviction to be immediately obedient. I pray you stop his/her feet from running from conviction. I pray that_____ will have a Damascus road experience where they encounter you fully and repent profusely and turn. I pray that _____ is quickly delivered from the idolatry of this fraternity/sorority. I command _____soul to hear on a greater height. I command the idols that for years have been speaking to ______ to go mute, blind, and deaf according to Psalms 115 while God speaks. As this happens, I call on warring angels to cast and curse the idols back to the pits of hell. Allow _____ to break free from wanting to be accepted or desiring demonic covenant. May the fear of the Lord come upon ________ and be the beginning of wisdom. I pray you give _____ the courage to tell their family, friends, line brothers or line sisters that they're leaving ________ (Fraternity or sorority name) and I thank you for alignment where that person will have the same conviction to leave the fraternity or sorority as well. I pray that as he/she immediately renounces and denounces, _____ will have a peace they do not understand. They will also see that they are not identified by the label of their sorority or fraternity, but that they are sons/daughters of God. Detach their identity from the fraternity or sorority or any social group. I thank you, God, that _______ will be grateful for revelation. They will not only tell those closest to them, but they will also tell the world and become an evangelist for this cause. I thank you that his/her grieving process will not be long, but a few minutes if that. The years that they were apart or lusted to be a part of the organization will feel like less than a minute and he/she will be able to part with and cut all ties...emotionally, financially, spiritually, physically; I pray for supernatural support. I pray he/she is met with other men/women who have left or want to leave. Even people still in, may they respect his/her decision and come to understanding that will bring the fear of the Lord to their heart. I pray he/she leans on his/her relationship with God first, then with others. I pray he/she will renounce this covenant and begin to pursue God with passion and unrelenting love. I pray _____ wins favor with all men and with you, oh God. I thank you that ___ ways will please you so even his/her enemies will be at peace with him/her. May _____ build a strong friendship/foundation and covenant with deep roots with you, God. I pray angels go before _____ and destroy any enemy trying to keep him/her tied to this sorority or fraternity. I pray _____ will have courage to look men in their faces and speak God's truth according to John 16:13 to power. God will send _____ opportunities and community to not replace the fraternity or sorority... but to be better. May _______ see a difference between Godly community and demonic soul ties to a fraternity or sorority. May _______ never feel lonely even when he's/she's alone, fill all voids that would lead _____ to demonic covenants just for community and to be loved. I decree ______ nor anyone on their bloodline will never return to any evil covenant, specifically of a fraternity or sorority. May you uncover all the witchcraft and occult practices and make him/her a leader in the charge for deliverance and knowledge from these organizations. God, wake up any dry bones that have died because of these adulterous ties to ______ (name fraternity or sorority). I stop any curses that are in action and call them to be destroyed with the hammer and with the fire of the Lord that breaks the rock into pieces. I rebuke any demonic gatekeeper in his/her family or friendships now and call for their immediate disarming. Neutralize them now and I command the gates to open NOW!! May cutting ties and renouncing legally stop all mental fatigue and torment or any other curse in action or to be time released. ______ will immediately see blessings instead of curses. Life instead of death. ______, hear the word of the Lord...IT'S TIME TO COME OUT! DEVIL RELEASE THEM NOW. Now that I, ______ (your name) with the Lord's backing contend in prayer for his/her soul... devil, you are in high treason. LOOSE HIM/HER AND LET HIM/HER GO, IMMEDIATELY! GOD, THANK YOU FOR HIS/HER RELEASE! Now as he/she is free, ______ will go and set the captives free! I bind any resentment towards me for my intercession or towards God. ______ will be grateful warfare went forth on behalf of their soul. I bind backlash and retaliation or sabotage to his/her mind, emotions, soul, body, health, family, destiny, relationships, marriage, jobs, and friends because ______ broke this evil covenant with the devil. Send His/her protective angels to guard them according to Psalms 91. Thank you, God, for their new beginning x2. Thank you for their deliverance!!! ______ is the bloodline repairer according to Isaiah 58:12.

REJOICE for it is already done, no matter how many times you have prayed this prayer, CHOOSE to believe God has heard you and when the time is right, He will honor your intercession.

Parents: Break any word curse you spoke over your children declaring they would be your legacy in a certain fraternity or sorority. Repent and cancel that in the assignment, with the blood of Jesus Christ.

"For if we sin willfully after we have received the knowledge of the truth, there no longer remains a sacrifice for sins, but a certain fearful expectation of judgment, and fiery indignation which will devour the adversaries." Hebrews 10:26-27 (NKJV)

Honorable Mention Idols

- Children

- Spouse

- Job

- Vices (shopping, smoking, sex, etc.)

- Pastor

- Drugs and Alcohol

- Sex

- _______________________________

- _______________________________

- _______________________________

- _______________________________

- _______________________________

- _______________________________

- _______________________________

- _______________________________

- _______________________________

- ______________________________

- ______________________________

- ______________________________

- ______________________________

- ______________________________

The Maintenance of Idolatry

Now that you have persevered through this book and before you congratulate yourself, I believe it's important for some of you to start or for others of you to continue the repentance and renouncing process. For some, this process is in tandem with a fast. For others, the simple declarations out of your mouth will do the justice of reversing years' worth of idolatrous ways–be led by the Holy Spirit. In addition, it's my mandated duty to give a warning. Matthew 12:43-45 (NKJV) says, "When an unclean spirit goes out of a man, he goes through dry places, seeking rest, and finds none. Then he says, 'I will return to my house from which I came.' And when he comes, he finds it empty, swept, and put in order. Then he goes and takes with him seven other spirits more wicked than himself, and they enter and dwell there; and the last state of that man is worse than the first. So shall it also be with this wicked generation." When you pray this prayer of deliverance, ensure when the spirit of (whatever you struggle with) comes back to proof and to test you, ensure your house is not empty, but filled with scripture and practical tools to walk out your deliverance. If you are not serious about being delivered from what is plaguing you, don't pray this prayer. Wait until, you're sure. I once heard a prophet of God say, "Deliverance is for the desperate" If you are not desperate yet, don't seek deliverance. In addition, deliverance must come with discipleship. Who will walk with you during the maintenance of your deliverance journey? Who will be the person or people that you can reach out to on those hard days when returning back to Egypt feels easier? Should you proceed with praying this prayer of deliverance, ensure you surround yourself with like-minded people in Christ, invested in the upgraded versions of you.

1. **Repent.** "God, forgive me for all my idolatry and my worship of other gods (list the idols you have worshipped). I am deeply sorry for the idolatry I have participated in, I now see how it has displeased you greatly. God, if there are hidden idolatrous sins, iniquities, and transgressions I have done that I don't know about or remember, bring them to my memory so I won't do it again; true repentance is what I desire. I also want to take this time to ask for forgiveness on behalf of my bloodline for their idolatrous ways. In Leviticus 26:40-42, you said we could ask for forgiveness on behalf of our forefathers, and you would be faithful to remember us, so God I'm asking for forgiveness and that you put my bloodline in remembrance today.

God, give me/us a legal pardon in the realm of the spirit... I'm agreeing with my adversary [satan] quickly, whatever sin my adversary said I've/my bloodline has done, I break legal right through repentance for these sins to continue speaking against me/my bloodline, in Jesus' name, amen."

2. **Renounce/Come out of agreement.** "God, I renounce, denounce and come out of agreement with any evil covenants that have been made through my idolatry and worship of other gods. God, as I renounce these evil covenants, in your mercy, show me these evil covenants I've made through my agreement with idolatry and worship of other gods so I can be a good steward with my forgiveness and never fall back into these evil covenants. In addition, God, in your mercy, show me the evil covenants that have held my bloodline captive for generations as well. By faith, I believe all you need is one to be the repairer of the broken walls (Isaiah 58:12) that will change the trajectory of a bloodline–I will be that one. God, I will be the gap stander you searched for in Ezekiel 22:30.

3. **Replace.** Now God, I ask you to replace the curses that have come as a result of the covenants made from idolatry. In scripture, we've seen that when people have been idolatrous, their land and everything that comes from their hands have been cursed. Today I'm asking for a reversal in the realm of the spirit. Where there's been early death, generational poverty, no marriages, sicknesses, diseases, barren women and barren land, contention and more. God this day replaces those curses with blessings–make the opposite true. Replace these generational curses with generational blessings. God, as I call for the replacing of these curses, help me to also remember that faith without works is dead. I speak these prayers by faith but teach me how to also work with Holy Spirit to do what it is you desire to see done in my life and bloodline to ensure these curses remain broken, in the name of Jesus, amen!"

4. **Rule, Reign, Dominion.** God, I have repented, renounced, and replaced these curses that have appeared in my life because of evil covenants through idolatry done by me or someone in my bloodline. While we don't deserve it, if it be pleasing to you and if it be your will, give me and my bloodline a Holy Pardon in the realm of the spirit. Instead of consequences, pardon us so we don't reap the evil harvest of what was done because of our idolatry or worship of other gods. I speak the remission of sins over the evil covenant and curse. Stop the curses in motion set to kill, steal and destroy us. Exonerate me and my bloodline. God, I give you rule, reign and dominion over me and my bloodline; have your way.

5. **Rebuke satan.** James 4:7(NKJV) says, "Therefore submit to God. Resist the devil and he will flee from you." Matthew 4:10 (NKJV) says, "Then Jesus said to him, "Away with you, Satan! For it is written, 'You shall worship the Lord your God, and Him only you shall serve.'"

Satan, you are now rebuked and I command you to flee from my life and my bloodline's life. You have no access to attack us in this area. The judge has rendered a verdict, *not guilty*. My bloodline and I have been absolved of any sins. The angels of the Lord have destroyed your evidence. As we stay in a repentant heart posture, should you try and attack in this area, you are in high treason. I decree and declare no trace or residue of any curse will be on my life or my bloodline. I declare, me and my bloodline are whole and healed. We will live and not die to declare the works of the Lord, in Jesus' name, amen.

6. **Bonus.** Please Note* Some curses can be broken from simple identification & repentance, while some curses are stubborn and have been on a bloodline for ages and won't come out unless through prayer and biblical fasting (no food, only water for a period of time, designated to you by God). This is according to Matthew 17:21 "This 'kind' won't come out unless through prayer and fasting." (Kind=*genos*, kindred, offspring, nation, family, stock, tribe, race, etc..).

In addition to the tool of prayer, I have provided above. It will prove advantageous to outline how the maintenance of idolatry could look and feel, as you walk out your deliverance.

Write out some steps for maintaining deliverance from idolatry:

____

____

____

____

____

____

____

The Reward for Idolatry

"Tearing down idols won't make you a hero, it'll make you hated."
-Prophetess Tiphani Montgomery

In chapter one, there were some rewards mentioned for the participation in idolatry. Instead of taking the time to list those again, I would just like to encourage you that if you have taken the necessary steps of repentance and have the desire to truly turn from past ways, there is no condemnation because you are in Christ. It's time for you to forgive yourself. For some of us, this is easy. Our idolatry will simply be a distant memory. For others of us, we will be reminded of our past idolatry daily. We can never get away from the consequences of our idolatry. This is when it would be helpful to ask God to help you forgive yourself. It will also be beneficial to accept the consequences of your past idolatry and to change your perspective surrounding it, try to view it as a blessing of a lesson rather than a burden of the past.

You Can No Longer Fellowship with Idolatry

"Although they know God's righteous decree that those who do such things deserve death, they not only continue to do these very things but also approve of those who practice them." Romans 1:32 (NIV)

Within any AA, NA, SLAA, OA meeting, before they close out with some encouragement, they might tell the attendees to change their community and create new habits. They would insist that for their proper recovery, it would be best to stop hanging with the same people that encouraged and enabled the addiction. It is the same for idolatry. If you had an idol of money for a season, it might be beneficial to unfollow crypto and/or investors on social media. If you made your emotions a god, it might be beneficial not to call on the one person that encourages you to engage in retail therapy or meaningless conversations when you're sad. Examine your circle. While your sin is never another grown person's responsibility, you can do your best to remove yourself so as to not be tempted to slip back into old ways. Take some time to think about the doorways of temptation. Really ponder on which ones need to be closed, and which ones can remain open. It's important to remember that all the door of sin needs is a little crack, a memory, a photograph, a text, a piece of clothing, a smell at best. You might even find that the same idolatrous activities you once participated in disgust you to think on and to witness. This disgust should not turn into haughtiness, but into intercession. The same prayers that turned you from your wicked ways will be the same prayers that free those still bound. You have no right to judge someone simply because they stayed in their sin longer than you.

Read Acts 17 as you reflect on closing the door to the idolatrous past.

Who and What You Agree with is Everything

"After this Jehoshaphat king of Judah allied himself with Ahaziah king of Israel, who acted very wickedly. And he allied himself with him to make ships to go to Tarshish, and they made the ships in Ezion Geber. But Eliezer the son of Dodavah of Mareshah prophesied against Jehoshaphat, saying, "Because you have allied yourself with Ahaziah, the Lord has destroyed your works." Then the ships were wrecked, so that they were not able to go to Tarshish." II Chronicles 20:35-37 (NKJV)

When I was in grade school, every year we would have a police officer come to the school to inform us about drugs and bullying. It always caught me by surprise when the officer would mention that a bystander was just as guilty as the bully, because of my lack of courage I was often a bystander. This taught me a very valuable lesson: that I would be held to the same consequences as the person committing the "crime" and that my silence was agreement. As an adult, I see just how my agreement is everything.

The enemy comes to disguise himself as a familiar spirit. Coming in the form of your friend or your family member in order to encourage you into agreement, but ultimately, you are coming into agreement with him (satan). Agreements that could result in life changing or even result in death. The same familiar spirit that has lurked around your bloodline for centuries and that has studied historical family patterns knows exactly what to do to make you fall into or back into idolatry. This could be agreement through words (Isaiah 59:21), actions (Genesis 24:2 & Jeremiah 33:20-26), visions or dreams (Genesis 15), through food (1 Corinthians 8), or even unknowingly (Joshua 9). We can easily find our way into covenants, this is why life with Holy Spirit is essential. When Holy Spirit says, "Don't sign that. Don't eat there. Don't give to that cause. Don't kiss them. Wake up and renounce that dream. Don't say that" it's important to listen. You will have to give an account for every idle word spoken out of your mouth. For every amen you came into agreement with and for every moment of silence that spoke a thousand words. I have worked my way into so many covenants just by idle/idol words spoken. Here's a few examples of ways I have spoken something over my life and saw it come to pass: "Just looking at that makes me sick." The next day I found myself sick. "It seems like I have more bills than money." That next payday I had more bills than money. "I can never do anything right." Everything I touched failed until I came out of agreement with this. "I guess I'll never get married." As I was praying for a husband, Holy Spirit revealed to me that because I had spoken this agreement over my life and my words had so much power, that He couldn't override what I had spoken to give me a marriage until I came out of agreement with those words.

Some things I chose to not come into agreement with: "It will take you at least three months to close on your home." Out of my mouth I said, "I don't come into agreement with that, it will take however long God needs it to." I found and closed on my home in less than a month. "Because you're dating long distance, your dating process will take longer." I came out of agreement with this statement the moment I heard it and asked God to be the timekeeper over my relationship. I met my husband in August, and we got married in November. "You will lose connections, money, and community leaving the sorority." I prophesied against this (Ezekiel 11:4) and to this day I have more money, more connections and more community. "Your marriage will be ______ and in your marriage you all will struggle with ______. My husband and I actively come out of agreement anytime someone wants to speak something negative over our marriage. This is not being "unrealistic", it's being the gatekeeper to your own life. If we're going to struggle or if something is going to happen, it's not going to be because of what we came into agreement with.

Most of these things spoken over me were by friends or family. They meant no harm, but in those moments, I remembered we don't argue against flesh and blood. It might have been my friend saying those things, but it was a spirit behind her that anticipated my agreement. I had to decide if I was going to be socially acceptable or if I was going to protect myself. It makes for socially awkward conversations when I am forced to kindly correct someone by coming out of agreement with what they attempt to speak over me, but this is necessary. Sometimes I'm even met with "It's not that big of a deal," or "Stop being so deep." I would rather be too deep than to be bound. I wouldn't want to imagine my life if I didn't have the courage to speak up for myself against people I love. I also have an understanding that I cannot expect someone to understand my plight when they themselves are riddled with invisible covenants because of their ignorance (Hosea 4:6). Please note, being conscious of what you come into agreement with is not to make you live in paranoia. This is simply an ear tuned to Holy Spirit, able to hear Him whenever He speaks.

Revelation 12:11

Now That You've Read This Book, Let's Get Into Action

"Have I therefore become your enemy because I tell you the truth?" - Galatians 4:16 (NKJV)

There's a step in the maintenance of deliverance that many people ignore–testimony. It's almost as if a silencing spirit comes to muzzle the mouths of the delivered. This spirit works in tandem with fear, shame and often invites whatever other spirit that specializes in keeping free people quiet. Revelation 12:11 says, "And they overcame him by the blood of the Lamb and by the word of their testimony, and they did not love their lives to the death" (NKJV). Satan doesn't want us to overcome him, he can do nothing to stop the blood of the Lamb, that is a finished work, but he does everything to silence a testimony–your testimony.

"Sharing your testimony will save your life, it saved Paul's life many times." - Deja Garner

In my daily attempt to stomp the devil out in my Timberland boots, I'll share my testimony of how God saved me from suicide ideations because of my idolatry and disobedience.

I alluded to this testimony in an earlier chapter entitled *Idolatry of Marriage*, so I'll spare the redundant details since they are written in that chapter. In short, due to my idol worship of marriage I found myself in a hotel room ready to take my life. The spirit of deception that works closely with idolatry led me to believe God had betrayed me. Feeling as if my God betrayed me and feeling as if the one person that was supposed to love me led me to believe a lie, I didn't want to live. Besides the deep sleep God swiftly carried me off to, the only other thing that kept me alive was my hope, my faith and my limited knowledge of God's character. In my years of Vacation Bible School, Sunday School, and Bible Study I was able to learn God's character. I knew His character wouldn't purposely hurt me because I was His beloved. I also knew that even with God's "betrayal" of me, there must have been a good reason. I was confident that since it wasn't good, it wasn't over. He had to be setting me up for the biggest breakthrough behind this pain. The racing thoughts paced in and out of logic and emotion. The emotional thoughts encouraged me to take my life, while the logical thoughts encouraged me to trace God's track record. My track record with God was a fist full of hope that I could cling to. The spirit of suicide invited by the spirit of idolatry and deception hovered over me like a cloud until God stepped in and rebuked them on my behalf. Ultimately, my hope and my relationship with God is what saved me from taking my own life. The next morning, life didn't seem so bleak. I had a lot to be grateful for. I was an idol worshipper who had found favor with the one and true living God, and in His mercy, did He spare my life. He could have easily let idolatry be the root cause of my early death, but He saw this moment. He saw me sharing my testimony in a book and on platforms that millions would read, listen to and see. He saw me giving Him the glory for delivering me from the claws of idolatry. I can't help but think He also saw you, He saw you reading this and by the spirit, He saw the chains breaking. He saw the deliverance through knowledge taking place. He saw you being freed and, in His mercy, did He spare my life for such a time as this. God, I thank you for your mercy.

The next and final testimony I'd like to share is how my disobedience, idolatry of money and ultimately a man led me to contemplate suicide for the second time in my life. I mentioned this in an earlier chapter entitled *Idolatry of Money*. It was 2023 and I was in the thick of unknown, but blatant idolatry. I was coming into a greater understanding of idolatry while also trying to resist the knowledge. The week of New Years Eve in 2022 spearheaded this idolatry–I met a man and fell into lust and this burning desire for him displeased God so well. In my last dating season at the top of 2022, God gave me a few commandments concerning my next dating season that in the matter of days with this man I broke. God said, "You are not to kiss this man, and the marriage bed is undefiled. Kayla, that means no naps because one thing will lead to another." It was easy to accept these stipulations with no man in sight. About ten months after these commandments, I met this man and broke them within less than a week. While we didn't have sex, we took a nap, but had God given us a few more days together who knows what would have happened. Out of nowhere, he breaks up with me on New Years Eve, and this sends me into a spiral. This spiral showed me I wasn't delivered from idolatry. I would go on for the next five months swerving in and out of idolatry. Showing God, I only wanted to serve Him, but the way my heart grieved from the pain of not being with this man was proof I was still an idol worshipper.

Now that you have the back story, let's jump forward.

"In faith" I believed this man and I would be together by April. I purchased two V.I.P tickets to a conference that I knew would bless us spiritually. A few weeks later, I heard the Lord tell me to purchase two general admission tickets. As I purchase the tickets, I hear the Lord say, "I will show you who to give these tickets to." A few weeks after the purchase, this couple was being prophesied to at my church and I heard the Lord say, "*Them*. That's who you are to give the tickets to." I know my role in the kingdom: I'm a serial sower and a kingdom financier. I ask God if He could take it a step further and provide them with a hotel and plane tickets to this conference in Texas. God delivers as He always does, so I asked them to meet me after church so I can speak with them about what God has done for them. They are elated and we are all preparing for the conference. In faith, I still believe this man will be able to attend the conference with me because in my mind, I'm believing we'll be together by then. I see no change in his actions, nor do I hear God say anything about him being mine or going to the conference (I didn't know I was still so deep in idolatry, but there were signs). One day in my bedroom I'm praying, and I hear from the Lord that I am supposed to give the V.I.P tickets to the couple and that I'm supposed to take the general admission tickets. Confused and offended, I cast it off as a suggestion and not a command from God. Depending on the situation, my convictions hit like a UFC fighter's knockout punch. Within the span of fifteen minutes, the conviction grew and began to pound in my head. I knew I was in disobedience, but pride wouldn't let me concede. The conviction was so heavy I remember holding my head between my knees and rocking because I felt I was going insane. The mental torment wasn't so much physical, but it was as if I wanted to get out of my head, but there was no way out. That's when the idea of suicide was brought to my attention. The torment persisted to the point where I wanted to bang my head against the wall to make the racing thoughts stop. What I didn't know then, but I know now was that because of idolatry, the spirit of suicide had a legal right to suggest. The enemy knew that in the tension of idolatry it would be a perfect time to kill me before I became a bigger threat to his kingdom. It's almost as if something took over my mind and begin to suggest ways, I could kill myself. Finally, through the racing thoughts and noises in my head I hear God command again, "Transfer the V.I.P tickets out of your name and into theirs." I immediately sent the email and requested the V.I.P tickets be transferred to them and the general admission tickets be transferred to the young man and I. As soon as the email was sent it was like I was levitated and then suddenly dropped to the ground, out of the mental chains. I could feel the literal peace wash over my mind again, I just laid there in a weepy silence for a while, grateful to have peace in my mind. Later, I asked the Holy Spirit to explain to me what happened, He said, "Why did it take all of that? When I ask you to do something, do it immediately." He then brought to my mind Saul's tormenting spirit (1 Samuel 16:14) and I was terrified. The great and mighty God had shown me, in the span of 15-30 minutes, a mind without the covering of His spirit. I was sent into a wild repentance and even to this day, I get chills when I think of this. Holding onto those V.I.P tickets was a representation of how I held onto the idol of that man. Releasing the tickets was the start of me releasing him. It was the start of the demonic idolatrous hold being released. In the end it all worked out. I didn't go to the conference with the man, because that wasn't God's plan. I went and sat in general admission. What I didn't know was that instead of an idolatrous relationship, God wanted to give me a covenant friendship. Had I been in V.I.P I never would have sat with her and built a connection. In addition, God didn't let that 2nd ticket go to waste. On the plane ride to the conference my new covenant friend met a woman traveling in faith. The woman heard the Lord say that if she went to the conference, He would have a ticket waiting on her. Before my friend got on the plane I told her I had a spare ticket, and I was looking to bless someone with it. When my new friend and this stranger arrived at the conference, I was able to bless her with a conference ticket that was always supposed to be hers. As for the man, thank God I dodged a bullet and as for the couple, they needed to be in V.I.P because they needed to see just how God felt about them. He would ask a stranger that attended their church to pay for their hotel, flights, and conference tickets–no strings attached. I'm confident when given the chance, they will go out and do the same.

I share these testimonies only to prove how sovereign God is. No matter how far gone I have been, the Lord, strong and mighty, always shows His hand. He always flexes His strength and I'm grateful to serve a God with real power. In addition, my hope is that because I have shared, this gives you permission to share your story. Sharing your testimony will save your life and those around you. I believe that every time you share, it will free you. The use of your voiceprint weakens satan's power and hold over you. It also disrupts the status quo of cowardice Christians that have more fear of the devil than God. Remembering who and whose you are. With a full understanding that you went through all of what you experienced not just for your evolution, but also for someone else. Because Jesus snatched the keys of death, hell and the grave, He gave us permission to snatch keys to sin that so easily ensnares us, ultimately to unlock our freedom, and hopefully to help someone else unlock theirs.

Protocols and Systems

"Discipline is a weapon against idolatry."

After 9/11, America began to put protocols in place in case anything like that ever happened again. After any type of school incident, a school puts additional protocols in place to ensure the safety of all. After distrust in a relationship, there are protocols created to secure and restore the relationship. After idolatry, there must be protocols introduced to your lifestyle to ensure you never fall back into the grasp of idolatry again. To put these protocols and systems in place might be trial and error, but when the enemy comes to proof your deliverance, it must be able to withstand his devices. Similar to a high-tech building, one button should be pressed, and the system goes into protection mode. This should be done in the early stages after deliverance from idolatry. System and protocol planning varies from person to person but is very necessary to have in place. While this should be contoured to your own experience and put in place with the help of Holy Spirit, here are a few protocols that have helped me:

- Learn to test every spirit, especially your own. (1 John 4:1)

- Learn to distinguish between your voice, God's voice and the enemy's voice. A lot of people say, "I heard God say..." When really because of the idols set up in their hearts, God allowed them to be deceived (Ezekiel 14:4). When a thought comes to my mind, I ask God blatantly, "Is this the idol speaking, you speaking or me?" On several occasions have I heard the Holy Spirit reason with me saying, "That's the idol, why would I encourage you to do such a thing?"

- Make it a part of your daily prayer to ask God to search your heart according to Psalms 139:23-24.

- Repent daily or hourly if necessary. As you repent, make it a part of your repentance to ask for forgiveness for idolatry, even if you don't feel it necessary. In addition, as you ask for forgiveness, also ask for the awareness and knowledge of what you are doing that is grieving God so you can stop doing it.

- An indication you're in idolatry is when it is the first thing you think about when you wake up and the last thing you think about when you go to sleep. When I was dating my now husband, because I had a past idol of marriage, I knew when I began to fixate on when we would marry and things concerning our future marriage, I had fallen back into idolatry. After repentance: I was willing to give up my relationship for God and that's when I knew the idolatry was gone.

Even though I really wanted to marry him, as a maintenance from idolatry, I knew if I needed to, my soul would survive without him as my husband. Only when I put our relationship under God's feet is when I could clearly hear God speak about our future.

- I once heard James Aladiran pose the question, "Are your angels bored?" and I felt so convicted because I knew my angels were bored out of their minds. A few months prior the Lord gave me a revelation to only pray the word God since His angels hearken to His word waiting to perform it (Psalms 103:20). God warned me against praying amiss (James 4:3) so the prayer strategy He gave me was to pray using scripture. For example, "God, in your word you said that you would deliver me in times of trouble, preserve me and keep me alive, and not let me be delivered into the hands of my enemies because I considered the poor. God, I consider the poor, so due to spiritual law, I'm asking you to bless me according to Psalms 41:1-4, in Jesus' name, amen!" Maintain your deliverance with prayers using scripture. Only the word of God is strong enough to keep the strongholds broken.

- Build up your prophetic walls. At this point in your life after idolatry, you're probably so preoccupied on never falling back into idolatry that you are neglecting your prophetic walls. God tells you something, but you can't or won't believe it because of the prophetic insecurity from the breach of idolatry. You must build these walls back up and strengthen them with the word of God. Get to the point where you can trust yourself with what you hear again. Ask God to help you trust yourself again. Ask Him to take you through a series of trainings that will build this muscle back up.

You Cannot Kill a Dead Man

"For if you live according to the flesh you will die; but if by the Spirit you put to death the deeds of the body, you will live." Romans 8:13 (NKJV)

This is a system and/or protocol that needs to be outlined on its own. Our flesh is always looking to be the main character. We are naturally idolatrous whores. Fasting the Biblical way silences and kills the flesh, allowing God to be louder than past idolatrous ways. This isn't a fast with the church once a year. This is a weekly lifestyle, a daily consecration to keep your flesh in check and subject to the will of God. Asking God to take away anything within you that has become an enemy to you. Insisting that He kills every enemy of your soul and enemy to your assignment. Willingly killing your flesh before it kills you. As fasting silences your flesh, you will be able to hear God more clearly. All while circumcising your heart of flesh as it is no longer a heart of stone.

Humility

"And whoever exalts himself will be humbled, and he who humbles himself will be exalted." Matthew 23:12 (NKJV)

"Therefore humble yourselves under the mighty hand of God, that He may exalt you in due time," 1 Peter 5:6 (NKJV)

In the Kingdom of God, it's important to remember that to go higher you must first go lower. In Matthew 18:4, Jesus explains that whoever humbles themself like a child is the greatest in the Kingdom of Heaven. There are so many that refuse to stay in a child's place because their flesh is the main character with pride directing the show. Humility costs more than pride. Humility is forgiving even when you're right. Humility is waiting patiently for God to vindicate you when you could have cleared your name years ago. Humility is the weapon you pull out to cut off anything that is unlike God. While in the process of maintenance from idolatry, in humility, you might have to schedule an apology tour. Under the influence of Holy Spirit's conviction, the people that tried to tell you about yourself that you ignored will need to be the first stop. With every apology, you sink deeper into humility. Wearing it like a cloak of protection. Even if your enemies wanted to, they couldn't humiliate the humble, because you couldn't get any lower than you are. As you get low, do the work to stay low; you've humbled yourself before the Lord had to do it. Don't let Leviathan, the king of all pride, exalt you out of God's will.

While you're walking in the spirit of humility, it's also helpful to remember that you're replaceable. Look at Saul and David, Vashti and Esther, Elijah and Elisha, Eli and Samuel, Moses and Joshua. He's a merciful God, but we should not confuse it for weakness. He has options, you are more than likely not His first choice, you're just the first one that said yes–humble yourself. He asked your great-great grandmother and your mother to surrender that idol on behalf of the bloodline, but they didn't have the faith to believe they could live without it–humble yourself. You simply were the one who, like David, was tired of the uncircumcised Philistine picking on your bloodline so you did something about it–humble yourself. Never think there aren't ten more behind you that aren't ready to take your place–be humble.

You Cannot Help Deliver if You Are Not Fully Delivered

"Examine yourselves as to whether you are in the faith. Test yourselves. Do you not know yourselves, that Jesus Christ is in you? —unless indeed you are disqualified. But I trust that you will know that we are not disqualified." - 2 Corinthians 13:5-6 (NKJV)

In order to help others you don't have to be perfect, but if you intend to rescue people from the enemy's camp, you cannot look like the enemy. Sometimes we develop this savior complex and the same way God saved us we want that for others. Not realizing it was a grace on our deliverance, it was Grandma's covenant prayers and fasting that broke the chains of bondage over our lives. Not understanding that, just like the Sons of Sceva, you carry no power. Inevitably, you will show up at the enemy's camp one way and flee seven ways (Deuteronomy 28:7). Upset with God because spiritual warfare is brutal, not realizing you microwaved your deliverance process when God needed you in a slow cooker to rid you of every city in Egypt. Doing what most would deem "good" work for the Kingdom of God, but because you are out of the timing and the will of God, your work is smoke in His nostrils. Causing harm and leaving a trace of blood on everyone you "help." When I left the sorority, I rushed my deliverance process. I wanted to be healed so badly; I painted over the cracks on the wall. Pretty soon that paint began to peel and the cracks widened, exposing all the areas I was too arrogant to think I needed healing in. People pleasing needed to be addressed, lack of discernment needed to be examined, the gods who sat on the throne of my heart needed to be de-throned. I found myself back-pedaling my deliverance. Yes, God planned for this, but who was unnecessary collateral damage because I rushed my deliverance process? There are thousands of souls attached to your deliverance, in due diligence, let God take His time on the operating table. When it's time, you will be launched into spheres that only a living God could orchestrate–all to reconcile souls back to Christ.

The Ministry of Reconciliation

"Now all things are of God, who has reconciled us to Himself through Jesus Christ, and has given us the ministry of reconciliation, that is, that God was in Christ reconciling the world to Himself, not

imputing their trespasses to them, and has committed to us the word of reconciliation." 2 Corinthians 5:18-19 (NKJV)

The ministry of deliverance is the ministry of reconciliation. You have been delivered from idolatry for a purpose. What does your reconciliation back to Christ mean to you?

____

____

____

____

____

____

____

____

You went through it so you can help others through it. What population or demographic are you called to help reconcile back to Christ? Hint: It might be the same demographic of people you once looked like.

____

____

____

____

____

____

____

____

____

Reward for Turning from Idolatry

In chapter one, I mentioned some rewards for turning from your idolatrous ways. I'd like to give Biblical examples of how God restored those who turned from the feet of their idols and made a conscious, yet faith-filled choice to choose God.

<u>Abraham:</u>

Context: Abraham's father was named Terah. Terah and his father, Nahor worshipped idols (Joshua 24:2). Many theologians also say that not only did Terah worship idols, but he made and sold them. Abraham, naturally growing up around this, probably cried out to God asking Him for something else, wondering if idol worship of false gods was all his life would be. I would even venture to think if Abraham thought on occasion, *The people around me tell me to bow down to these fertility gods. I wonder if my wife would still be barren if I did?* I imagine after seventy-five years, he had enough. Judging by the quickness of Abraham's obedience to go and follow the Lord, I know this happened at an appointed time. When the Lord called Abraham to leave the family he knew and go to a place the Lord would direct him to, I'm sure Abraham had reservations, but he was obedient. In Abraham's obedience to God's call to go, he turned his back on his family gods and followed the one and true living God. Abraham's reward exists to this day; a once childless man, now with many descendants—he is the father of our faith.

SN: I'd like to point out how Abaham was not perfect: He was a liar and sometimes a coward, but he was faithful. More importantly he spoke in God's love language—obedience.

Ruth:

"But Ruth replied, "Don't urge me to leave you or to turn back from you. Where you go I will go, and where you stay I will stay. Your people will be my people and your God my God. Where you die I will die, and there I will be buried. May the Lord deal with me, be it ever so severely, if even death separates you and me."" Ruth *1:16-17 (NIV)*

Context: Due to idolatry, the Lord caused a famine to fall on the land of Judah, because of this Elimelech took his wife, Naomi and two sons to Moab. Moab was a country that was known for the worship of idols, specifically the god of Chemosh (1 Kings 11: 7 & 33). While in Moab, his two sons met their wives, Ruth & Orpah. After the death of Naomi's husband and her two sons she decided, she would return to the land she knew and loved Bethlehem. Orpah, one of her daughters-in-law, decided to stay in Moab, go back to her home and start over. Ruth, however, clung to her mother-in-law and decided to journey with Naomi back to her land. Theologians believe that during this time of Ruth being married to Mahlon, Naomi's son, Ruth was able to see the God in Naomi. It was here that Ruth saw the difference between the god she served all her life versus the God of Judah. I believe that God was specific in using this method of evangelizing. He took intimate moments of a mother-in-law/daughter-in-law relationship and used it to win over a soul. When Ruth cried out to her mother-in-law in Ruth 1:16-17, she not only sealed her fate with her mother-in-law, but she also sealed her fate with the Lord when she explicitly told Naomi she would serve her God. Turning from the idolatry of her ancestral land, this day, she chose who she would serve. This bold move of faith sent her on a path of being redeemed from idolatry. Ruth would go on to marry the Kinsman Redeemer of the family, Boaz. Together they would have Obed, Obed would have Jesse, and Jesse would go on to have David. Out of the lineage of David, our Lord and Savior would come, the ultimate Kinsman Redeemer. Only a merciful God could redeem someone born into idolatry, a childless widow, a Moabitess and place them into the lineage of His only son. Naomi also received redemption, she named herself, "Mara" because God had caused her to be very bitter (Ruth 1:20). God didn't allow her story to end there. When Naomi chose to return to the land of her God and leave the land of idolatry her husband brought her to, we see the hand of the Lord directing her to restoration. When Ruth gave birth to Obed, the women of the town exclaimed how blessed Naomi was, saying that Ruth had been better to her than 7 seven sons (Ruth 4:15).

I've often heard the quote by William J Toms, "Be careful how you live. You may be the only Bible some person ever reads." In the book of Ruth this proves to be true. The way Naomi lived her life for God encouraged Ruth to turn from her idolatrous family history and serve God. How are you living in front of people, specifically the people closest to you? You can fool strangers and followers, but you can't fool the ones that see how you live when there are no cameras. As you are delivered and maintain your deliverance from idolatry, like Naomi, who are you bringing with you to freedom? Not by force or by shame, but by showing the love of God and by your lifestyle.

By Faith

Write a Hebrews 11 "By Faith" statement:

By faith, I *Inserts name* renounced the idolatry of...I did this because...I had been bound since... By faith I.... By faith I...By faith I saw...By faith I heard...

See Hebrews 11 for examples.

God Loves You

As this book comes to an end, the most important thing I want you to know is how much God loves you and how jealous He is over *you*. You serve a God that doesn't play around about *you*. In fact, He thought you were to die for. That's why He couldn't bear the thought of you being and staying in idolatry. God sacrificed His only son to reconcile *you* back to Him. As you pray the prayer below, pray it knowing that because you are made in His image, like any good cultivator, He must take away everything that is not like Him. He must strip all earthly things away and refine you, not as silver and gold, but in the furnace of affliction (Isaiah 48:10). He will walk this journey alongside you as the old passes away and you become new (2 Corinthians 5:17). Understand that there are so many that will never release their idols. Inevitably, they will die and be buried with their idols; they've chosen their fate and they are content. Some of them might even read this book and because of the deceptive veil over their eyes, won't be convicted, but not you. You see the error of your ways, and you are ready to choose the one and true living God. You are ready to die to yourself in order to live for God. Rest in the fact that on this journey to a fleshly death, to a cultural death, to a worldly death, you will be accompanied by the one who formed you in your mother's womb. He will comfort you if you're the only one speaking out against idolatry. Jehovah Gibbor will fight for you if all your friends and family turn on you for publicly denouncing their god. All of Heaven is backing you because you serve a covenant keeping God–He will never let you out-sacrifice Him. I'm so proud of you for choosing the narrow gate (Matthew 7:13-14). Don't ever stop choosing the narrow gate. *Idolatry* might have made you do it, but your love for God, made you stop doing it.

A Prayer:

Heavenly Father, I thank you for not being a man that you should lie nor the son of man that you should repent. In your word you said, if I made my bed in hell, you would be there. God, I have made my bed in hell and there you were—Yeshua; you rescued me and threw me a party (Psalms 91:15 (MSG)). What more can I ask for when I have a God as merciful as you? Thank you for calling me redeemable even after I chose the pigpen over the palace. Thank you for setting a standard of holiness and requiring I be set apart to serve you. Thank you for not being like those other gods that are okay with open relationships. Thank you for demanding my monogamy in a world where having multiple gods is normal. Thank you for being a bridegroom that desires his bride to be without spot or wrinkle. More importantly, thank you for giving us this example in

Jesus to show us it's possible. God, now I want to ask for your forgiveness. Forgive me for falling into the trap of idolatry. I became part of this world and for that, I offer my deepest apologies. Time and time again, you've watched me flirt with other gods and worship graven images and, in your mercy, you let me live. My wages for sin is death, but in your mercy did you allow me time to repent, rather than dropping dead in my idolatry. I want to also take the time to repent on behalf of my bloodline–chances are this idolatrous pattern didn't start with me. I can't say who exactly introduced these idolatrous ways into my family, but I am eternally honored you would bestow the task upon me to end it. I wear this badge with honor, and I don't take it lightly. As the repairer of the breach in my family, as the minister of reconciliation for my bloodline, I ask you for forgiveness on behalf of a family member who is convinced they're not wrong, on behalf of a family member that is too prideful to repent, on behalf of a family member that is oblivious to their idolatry. In my repentance on behalf of them, I'm requesting you put my bloodline in remembrance and turn their hearts back to you according to Leviticus 26:40-42. In your mercy, give them time to repent, a chance to get it right with you. Don't give them over to their reprobate minds and to their delusions; Father please don't take your grace from their lives.

Before I speak to the idolatry that has plagued my life. I speak to the demonic patterns that helped me into idolatry, and I rebuke you out of my life. Thank you, God, for taking the veil of deception off my eyes to notice the patterns and lack of discipline that is priming me as a candidate for idolatry. God, take away my heart's desire for the things that displease you. Rid my heart of pride that two steps back and forth over the line of sin whenever I feel like it. Father, you told the 10 lepers that as they went, they would be healed. Father, as I go, cleanse my ears, my heart, my mouth, and eyes to only hear you, love you, speak to you, and see you. Keep my heart in the palm of your hand. Help me to hide your words in my heart so I may not ever sin against you. Allow the fallow ground of my heart to remain tilled. Keep my heart from becoming stoney, when a fleshly heart is what you desire. Father, allow my new position to be at your feet; there, I'm safe from flying arrows of idolatry. As I walk out my maintenance, give me wisdom and strategy to remain delivered and to go and help others. Father, I offer my life–do with it what you will. In closing, God, I ask that you make a covenant with me. I ask that as I walk out my deliverance from idolatry all the days of my life that you keep my children and the next generation of my bloodline to 1000 generations. Father, I don't want them to end up where I was. I'm asking that when they are faced with the choice to worship idols, may a conviction and a word from the Holy Spirit rise on the inside of them leading them to the righteous path instead of a path of destruction. Father, you told David that because He did so much work for your Kingdom, His son would have a life of rest (1 Chronicles 22:6-9). Abba, that is what I am requesting for my children and the next generation in my bloodline to 1000 generations–give them a life of rest from the temptation of idolatry and the desire to be idolatrous. I will continue my work for you and serve you with my life until you call me to eternity. While you owe me nothing, while I deserve every piece of death, hell and the grave, in your mercy, would you honor my request. Again, I say, Idolatry made me do it, but may my love for you, O God, make me stop doing it, in Jesus' name, amen.

About The Author

Kayla Fointno Richardson is a faith-based author of children's and adult books. She currently resides in Tulsa, Oklahoma with her husband, working as a Mental Health Therapist. Before graduating from North Carolina A&T State University, Kayla spent eight years in South Korea as an Army Brat, an experience that shaped her worldview and love for diverse cultures. Kayla is passionate about making mental health services accessible to everyone, regardless of socioeconomic status. When she's not writing, leading therapy sessions, teaching, or spending time with family and friends, she enjoys reenacting her favorite plays and screenplays, and even writing her own. Filmmaking has long been a passion, and she dreams of one day producing, acting, and directing her own projects. In the meantime, she finds joy in supporting other authors on their self-publishing journeys.

You can find Kayla in any of these ways:

www.booksbykjf.com

booksbykjf@gmail.com

@booksbykjf

@kayla_jf

Or scan the QR code:

Other books by the author:

We're Moving, Again

Good Different

Hey King's Kid

Waiting Well: Maximizing the Journey of Singleness

God Says Journal

All books can be found at www.booksbykjf.com

For questions please email booksbykjf@gmail.com